D1570402

Alejo Carpentier

Twayne's World Authors Series
Latin American Literature

David Foster, Editor

Arizona State University

TWAS 756

ALEJO CARPENTIER
(1904–1980)
Photograph courtesy of
Roberto González Echevarría

Alejo Carpentier

By Donald L. Shaw
University of Edinburgh

Twayne Publishers • Boston

Alejo Carpentier

Donald L. Shaw

Copyright © 1985 by G. K. Hall & Company
All Rights Reserved
Published by Twayne Publishers
A Division of G. K. Hall & Co.
A publishing subsidiary of ITT
70 Lincoln Street
Boston, Massachusetts 02111

Book Production by Elizabeth Todesco
Book Design by Barbara Anderson

Printed on permanent/durable acid-free
paper and bound in the United States of
America.

Library of Congress Cataloging in Publication Data

Shaw, Donald Leslie, 1930–
    Alejo Carpentier.

    (Twayne's world authors series; TWAS 756.
Latin American literature)
    Bibliography: p. 139
    Includes index.
    1. Carpentier, Alejo, 1904–
—Criticism and interpretation.
    I. Title.   II. Series: Twayne's world authors series; TWAS 756.
    III. Series: Twayne's world authors series. Latin American literature)
PQ7389.C263Z88   1985   863   84–25297
    ISBN 0–8057–6606–5

Contents

About the Author

Donald L. Shaw graduated M.A. from the University of Manchester, England, and gained the Ph.D. from Trinity College, Dublin, where he taught for two years. Subsequently he taught at the University of Glasgow and the University of Edinburgh, where he currently holds a Personal Chair in Latin American studies. He has been Visiting Professor at Brown University and at the University of Virginia. Among his numerous publications are short critical guides to works by Rómulo Gallegos and Jorge Luis Borges, and *Nueva narrativa hispanoamericana* (Madrid: Cátedra, 1981) on the "Boom" and the post-"Boom" in modern Spanish American fiction.

Preface

The emergence during and after the 1950s of a group of world-class Spanish American novelists (what has come to be called the "Boom" in Spanish American fiction) has been a major novelty in recent Western literature. The Cuban novelist Alejo Carpentier was one of the main figures of the Boom and his work illustrates many of the features we associate with it. These include a new vision of Spanish American reality past and present, a deep awareness of the potential tragedy of the human condition, a greater readiness to explore human sexuality and to incorporate humor into the novel, and the development of exciting innovatory narrative techniques.

More especially we associate with Carpentier as an individual "new novelist" his discovery and popularization of the idea of the marvelousness of Spanish American reality (to which Gabriel García Márquez was to pay tribute in his Nobel Prize acceptance speech) and his obsessive interest in time, which affects both the content and the structure of his novels. As a writer much of whose formative period was spent in France, he had at first to struggle to gain acceptance as a genuinely Spanish American novelist. In 1959, after establishing himself in the forefront of the new novel in the subcontinent, he created something of a sensation by returning from Venezuela, where he had been living for more than a decade, to Cuba, where he strongly supported the regime of Fidel Castro. Criticism of his work has since been beset with partisan prejudice. Nevertheless, at the time of his death in 1980 he was unanimously regarded as a leading figure in Spanish American letters. His works have been widely translated, while a dozen or so books and collections of essays, as well as hundreds of articles and reviews, attest to the interest of critics.

At the time this book was in preparation no single, adequate critical work dealing with the whole of Carpentier's fiction had been published. My primary aim, therefore, was to present an overview of his entire production. In trying to fulfill this aim it was necessary to steer a careful course between extremes of critical interpretation and to endeavor to offer a balanced appraisal of Carpentier's development from his earliest work, through his discovery of the "mar-

velous real," to his last, openly Marxist stance. During the writing
I have tried to introduce appropriate qualifications and reservations
and to do justice to different approaches, but the critical conclusions
are my own.

I owe grateful thanks to Roberto González Echevarría both for
providing me with the frontispiece photograph of Carpentier and
for the immense contribution that he and Klaus Müller-Bergh are
making to Carpentier studies. Every subsequent scholar is in their
debt. Additionally my thanks are due to Salvador and Pamela Bacarisse for the ungrudging loan of essential materials that would
have otherwise been difficult to obtain.

Donald L. Shaw

University of Edinburgh

Chronology

1904   Alejo Carpentier born in Havana, Cuba, 26 December, son of Jorge Julián Carpentier, French architect, and Lina Valmont, Russian language teacher.

1912   During early education in Cuba, returns with his parents to Europe and studies for three months at the Licée Jeanson de Sailly in Paris.

1916   Earliest attempts at writing. At this time living in the countryside near Havana.

1922   Begins study of architecture at Havana University. His father abandons the family. To assist financially he leaves University and embarks on career as journalist. Second visit to France.

1922   Journalism. Participates in avant-garde cultural groups such as the Grupo Minorista. Involved in political protest. Discovers Joyce, Picasso, Stravinsky, and other innovatory figures. Organizes concerts of modern music.

1926   First trip to Mexico. Friendship with revolutionary painter Diego Rivera. Signs a democratic and anti-imperialist manifesto against the regime of Gerardo Machado (1925–1933).

1927   Helps to found *Revista de Avance*. Imprisoned for political protest. Writes first draft of *Ecue-Yamba-O*.

1928   Leaves Cuba surreptitiously for France. Stages in Paris *Yamba-O* (a burlesque tragedy). Contributes articles regularly to *Social* and *Carteles* in Cuba. Undergoes deep influence of surrealism: friendship with Breton, Aragon, Tzara, Picasso, de Chirico, Villa-Lobos, and others.

1930   Founds shortlived literary magazine *Imán*.

1933   Completes final version of *Ecue-Yamba-O* and publishes it in Madrid. Now working in sound-effects and music department of French radio and directing a recording company (Foniric) specializing in literary recordings and recordings of avant-garde composers. December: "Histoire de lunes" published in *Cahiers du Sud*.

1934   During trip to Madrid makes friends with Lorca, Alberti, Salinas, Bergamín, and other leading writers.

1935   June: attends First Congress of (Anti-Fascist) Writers in Defense of Culture in Paris.

1937   Attends Second Congress in Republican Madrid, along with Vallejo, Guillén, Malraux, Paz, Langston Hughes, and others.

1939   Returns to Cuba by way of Belgium, Holland, and United States. Edits Havana journal *Tiempo Nuevo*. Later works as musicologist at Cuba's National Conservatory of Music. Works for Cuban radio stations. Marriage to Lilia Esteban.

1942   Works on uncompleted novel *El clan disperso,* material from which was later incorporated into *El siglo de las luces* and *La consagración de la primavera*.

1943   Makes trip to Haiti, which was to influence writing of *El reino de este mundo* and *El siglo de las luces*.

1944   Begins work on *El reino de este mundo*. Accepts contract for *La música en Cuba*. Publishes "Oficio de tinieblas" and "Viaje a la semilla."

1945   August: moves to Caracas, Venezuela. Works in radio (and later TV) advertising. Some journalism and teaching.

1946   *La música en Cuba* and "Los fugitivos" published.

1947   July: makes trip by air to interior of Venezuela, which is to influence writing of *Los pasos perdidos*.

1948   September: second trip to interior by bus and boat.

1949   *El reino de este mundo* published in Mexico.

1952   "Semejante a la noche" published in Cuba.

1953   January: finishes writing *Los pasos perdidos,* published that year.

1954   Extract of *El acoso* published in Cuba.

1955   During brief stay in Guadalupe discovers historical figure of Victor Hughes, later a major character in *El siglo de las luces*.

1956   *El acoso* published in Buenos Aires.

1958   *Guerra del tiempo* ("Viaje a la semilla," "El camino de Santiago," "Semejante a la noche," and *El acoso*) published. Makes trip to French Caribbean islands and obtains more material for *El siglo de las luces*.

1959   July: following success of the Cuban Revolution returns to Cuba from Venezuela. *El siglo de las luces* now almost complete.

1961   Trip to Czechoslovakia, East Germany, Poland, Russia, and China. Important speech, "Literature and Political Consciousness."

1962   *El siglo de las luces* published.

1962   Directs *Editorial Nacional de Cuba* and organizes important book festivals. Works for Cuban radio.

1964   *Tientos y diferencias* (essays) published.

1965   May: Finishes *El derecho de asilo*. May–June: "Los advertidos" published. Makes lecture tour of French universities.

1966   Removed from directorship of Editorial Nacional. Appointed Cuban Cultural Attaché in Paris. Lectures in various European countries as well as Morocco and Russia.

1967   Important speech in Geneva, "The Social Role of the Novelist," later included in the second (1967) edition of *Tientos y diferencias*. *El derecho de asilo* published both in Spanish and in French.

1970   *La ciudad de las columnas* republished from *Tientos y diferencias* as a book with copious illustrations.

1974   *El recurso del método* and *Concierto barroco* published. His seventieth birthday feted in Cuba.

1975   Awarded honorary doctorate by the University of Havana. Returns to Caracas to deliver an important series of lectures, later published as *Razón de ser* (Caracas, 1976). Mexico awards him Alfonso Reyes Prize. Also receives Cerro del Duca Prize. *Letra y solfa* (selected journalistic articles) published in Buenos Aires.

1976   Elected Honorary Fellow of the University of Kansas. Trips to Bucharest and London.

1978   January: *Les portes du soleil* (music drama; words by Carpentier) performed in Paris. *La consagración de la primavera* published. Receives Miguel de Cervantes Prize from King Juan Carlos in Madrid, 4 April.

1979   *El arpa y la sombra* published. Receives Prix Medici.

1980   Dies 24 April at his home in Paris (51 bis Av. de Ségur). Buried in Cuba in the Necropolis de Colón. Leaves unfinished his memoirs and a novel on Marx's son-in-law Paul Lafargue.

Chapter One
The Apprenticeship
Early Life

Alejo Carpentier was born on 26 December 1904 in downtown Havana.[1] His father, Jorge Julián Carpentier, an architect, was French. His mother, Lina Valmont, a teacher of languages, was of Russian origin. The couple had emigrated from France to Cuba in 1902. Both were extremely musical, Jorge Carpentier having studied the cello for a time with Casals. Alejo inherited their love of music and before emerging as a novelist seemed destined to make his mark as a musicologist and music critic. He also inherited from his parents an almost perfect command of French, which was to prove important in his career. He was asthmatic as a child and spent much of his boyhood in the countryside close to Havana, with intervals of schooling in the city. In 1912 he accompanied his parents on an extensive trip to Europe and attended the Lycée Jeanson de Sailly in Paris for three formative months. By early adolescence he was a competent pianist and had begun to read avidly, progressing from the usual adventure stories to Balzac, Flaubert, and Zola. At fifteen he was already trying his hand at short stories imitating Anatole France. At secondary school he was an average pupil and remembered himself as rather shy and lonely, devoting much of his free time to music and reading and a favorite pony. In 1921 he joined the School of Architecture of the University of Havana, but the break-up of his parents' marriage compelled him to abandon his studies and find work. He turned to journalism and worked as a columnist for various Cuban newspapers, especially *Carteles* and *Social,* until 1932 when, by now in Paris, he began a second career as a radio sound-technician and producer. But almost to the end of his life he was to remain devoted to journalism. Between 1945 and 1959, for instance, while living in Caracas he produced more than four thousand newspaper articles in addition to working in an advertising agency and writing fiction.

While earning his living as a journalist in his early twenties
Carpentier was making friends with many of the younger Cuban
writers and composers and participating in the activities of the
Grupo Minorista, which was trying to stir up the stagnant waters
of Cuban culture. Along with this went a degree of political protest
against the regimes of Alfredo Zayas and later of Gerardo Machado.
In 1927 Carpentier helped to found the influential avant-garde
magazine *Revista de Avance* (1927–30), which was devoted to na-
tionalism, radicalism, and above all to new ideas in the arts. He
also signed the important literary and political manifesto of the
Minorista group, which advocated a struggle for the revision of false
and worn-out values, for new art in its various manifestations, for
the reform of public education, for the economic independence of
Cuba, for resistance to yankee imperialism, for rejection of one-man
political dictatorships in the world, in the Americas, and in Cuba,
and for Latin American friendship and unity. In consequence he
and others fell under suspicion of having subversive as well as ul-
tramodern cultural ideas; he was accused of Communist sympathies
and imprisoned. During some six weeks in custody he began writing
what was to become his first novel, *Ecue-Yamba-O*. Released under
police surveillance he returned to journalism and, with his friend
the composer Amedeo Roldán, organized a series of concerts that
included music by new figures such as Poulenc and Malipiero as
well as Stravinsky, whom Carpentier greatly admired. But he was
in danger of rearrest and in 1929, with identification papers borrowed from a friend, he left Cuba surreptitiously for France, where
he was to live for the next eleven years.

The Background to *Ecue-Yamba-O*

About the time Carpentier was helping to found the *Revista de
Avance,* signs of a change in Spanish American fiction were beginning
to appear. The major novelists of the immediately preceding period,
who included such figures as Mariano Azuela (Mexico), Eduardo
Barrios (Chile), José Eustasio Rivera (Colombia), and Rómulo Gallegos (Venezuela), had faced a double imperative. On the one hand
they had felt compelled to break away from the earlier tendency to
imitate European (and especially French) late-nineteenth-century
novelists and create a pattern of fiction that was essentially American. It was to deal with the human condition as it was in Latin

America and specifically with the struggle to civilize the great empty interior, the plains, the jungle, the high mountain regions, and the Latin American temperament itself, with its long record of bloodshed and violence. But the second part of the imperative was the need to keep abreast of European, and before long North American, fictional techniques. Here they are sometimes held to have failed. What we have to recognize, however, in relation to Carpentier and his generation is not that these writers were technically inadequate (which is untrue). Rather, preoccupied as they were with the discovery and expression of a truly Latin American reality, they tended to see that reality as unambiguous, accepting that what they saw around them on the pampa, on the *llano,* in the jungles of Amazonia, or on the battlefields of the Mexican Revolution was really real. Their fault, if it was a fault, was to continue the great tradition of the novel of observation and to adjust their techniques accordingly.

In the River Plate region, where the signs of a change were most visible, 1926 was a peak year for this *criollista* novel, whose primary aim was to depict what was distinctively unique in Latin American man in his own local environment. Ricardo Güiraldes published what is perhaps the most famous of all such works, *Don Segundo Sombra;* Enrique Larreta published *Zogoibi* and Horacio Quiroga, the great Uruguayan writer of short stories set in the Misiones jungle, brought out *Los desterrados* (The exiled ones). But also in 1926 Roberto Arlt published his first novel, *El juguete rabioso* (The furious toy), with its important shift of background from the pampa and the forest to the city and from the theme of man's struggle with his environment to that of the absurdity of the human condition. Before long Macedonio Fernández was to begin his demolition of realism in literature and was already a major formative influence on the young Jorge Luis Borges.

Elsewhere the change was of a different kind. Inevitably one of the features of the *criollistas'* exploration of (especially) rural Latin America had been the gradual rediscovery of the indigenous Indian and *mestizo* population of Mexico and the Andean countries as a source of fictional material. But until the 1930s the role of the native inhabitants of Latin America tended to remain marginal, as in Gallegos's *Doña Bárbara,* where in spite of the symbolism of the mixing of races (such as Carpentier himself was later to use in the presentation of Rosario in *Los pasos perdidos {The Lost Steps}*), the hero marries a white girl. Or else, as in the Indianist novel, the

presentation was sentimentalized and the Indians were seen from
the outside in an old-fashioned way as picturesque and exotic. In
the 1930s, however, the pattern changed to one of greater realism,
and especially to indignant denunciation of the oppression of the
native population by the white landowners and authorities, that is,
to what is now called Indigenism.

This was not the full extent of the change, for at the same time
two major writers appeared who were to transform the presentation
of the Indians in Spanish American fiction: José María Arguedas in
Peru and Miguel Angel Asturias in Guatemala. What is significant
about both writers is that, while retaining a powerful element of
denunciation in their novels about the Indians, they began to present
these last (though still from the outside, since neither was a true
Indian) in a far more authentic way, with strong emphasis on their
magical and animistic outlook. In particular, Asturias's *Cuculcán*
(1930) is not unlike some of Carpentier's earliest work, such as his
ballet-scenario "El milagro de Anaquillé" (The miracle of Anaquillé,
1927).

Without any doubt, Carpentier's work up to and including the
final version of *Ecue-Yamba-O* in 1933 marks the appearance in Cuba
of an equivalent of this later phase of Indigenism. For this reason,
despite his subsequent rejection for many years of *Ecue-Yamba-O* and
the patronizing view that some critics have taken of it, the first
phase of Carpentier's work cannot be lightly dismissed. Cuban fiction in the late 1920s and early 1930s has been justly described as
in line with "the most pedestrian of realisms."[2] The leading novelists
were Carlos Loveira (1882–1928) and Miguel de Carrión (1875–
1929). The latter Carpentier has descibed as the only important
writer at that time in Cuba. Both were writers in the naturalist
tradition.

It is clear that Carpentier was determined from the outset of his
career to break with this tradition. Nor was the direction lacking.
We must remember his strong musical affiliations and in particular
his admiration for Stravinsky. In the 1920s avant-garde composers
from Stravinsky himself in Europe to Aaron Copeland in North
America were passing through a strongly nationalistic phase, which,
combined with the influence of the *Revista de Avance,* could hardly
have failed to affect the young Carpentier's outlook. The equivalent
in Cuba of the neoindigenism of Asturias and Arguedas on the
mainland was the Afro-Cuban movement. It encompassed not only

poetry and fiction but also music and painting, and Carpentier was right in the middle of it. "El milagro de Anaquillé" (1927) and "La Rebambaramba" (1928) were Afro-Cuban ballets with scenarios by Carpentier and music by his friend Roldán, who also set to music Afro-Cuban poems by Nicolás Guillén and the Puerto Rican Luis Palés Matos. In Paris in 1928 Carpentier staged *Yamba-O*, an Afro-Cuban burlesque with music by M. F. Gaillard and soon after was writing Afro-Cuban poems that were later to figure in important anthologies. At the same time he began to collect paintings by the then little known Afro-Cuban painter Wilfredo Lam.

Afro-Cubanism meshed with the search, begun in earlier Latin American writing, for local authenticity and national roots. Carpentier was to remark later that it offered "the possibility of expressing criollism with a new notion of its values" and that it represented a "renewed national awareness."[3] But there is another authenticity that is at once part of the same quest and yet different. This is the authenticity of primitivism. Roberto González Echevarría has argued that Afro-Cubanism, as well as being part of the struggle to find and express what is autonomously Latin American, is also part of a widespread rebellion against the heritage of a Europe seen in Spenglerian terms as culturally bankrupt.[4] Oswald Spengler's *The Decline of the West* had appeared in Spanish in 1923. He praised younger, more spontaneous, less intellectualized cultures and art forms and was thus highly relevant to Afro-Cubanism.

The popularization of Spengler's ideas in Cuba and elsewhere in Latin America followed the growth of the belief among artists and writers in the West generally that direct figurativeness in the visual arts and realism in literature were now things of the past. Thus primitivism, which was welcome to the nationalistically minded since it appeared to offer the prospect of finding new and specifically Latin American values, was also acceptable to the avant-garde because it held out the possibility of renewing artistic forms. In fact it was the avant-garde both in Europe and America that took up primitivism as a source of innovation. But we must recall that Afro-Cubanism, for all its differences, was related to neoindigenism and hence retained a strong element of social protest. So at the beginning of his career, in "El milagro de Anaquillé" and the far more important *Ecue-Yamba-O*, Carpentier found himself pursuing three aims that even a more seasoned writer would have found it hard to render compatible with one another. These were the search for what was genuinely and uniquely Cuban, the struggle to innovate formally, and the impulse to protest, especially about foreign economic exploitation. Not surprisingly critics have agreed with Carpentier that *Ecue-Yamba-O* is not a fully successful novel. An introduction to some of its themes is provided by "El milagro de Anaquillé." In this ballet-scenario a grotesque parody of a North American businessman/film director attempts to take over a fragment of Cuban scenery, with a couple of huts, as a backdrop for a film. Contemptuously dismissing the possibilities of the local poor-white peasant dancers as film material, he covers the huts with American billboard advertisements, adds a pseudoskyscraper, and brings on his own Hollywood-style dance act. He is interrupted, however, by the arrival of a group of black sugar-cane cutters who, after destroying his posters, perform an initiation ceremony accompanied by dancing. This fascinates the North American and he attempts to incorporate it into his film. When the blacks react angrily to his dancers, he attackes the *Iyamba,* or black shaman, who is directing the ceremony, but is defeated and humiliated by the intervention of two *Jimaguas* (twin black figures representing supernatural forces). The blacks, with the aid of magic, defeat the vulgar commercialism and arrogance of the white American intruder. We notice, then, Carpentier's anti-imperialist protest, his use of proletarian and black characters, and his interest in local beliefs.

Ecue-Yamba-O

Set at first in a rural sugar-producing area of Cuba after the abrupt fall in sugar prices in 1920 had led to economic crisis, *Ecue-Yamba-O* (the title means "Lord, praised be thou") is the story of a young black, Menegildo Cue. In love with another man's woman, he knifes his rival and is imprisoned in Havana as a result. On his release he joins a criminal secret society and dies in a scuffle with another gang. From the outset the reader is conscious of the same basic conflict as in "El milagro de Anaquillé." The novel begins with a deliberate contrast between the menacing concrete block of the sugar-grinding mill, which dominates the surrounding area, and the traditional, preindustrial, earth-centered outlook of Usebio, Menegildo's father. Emphasis on the inhumanity of the conditions imposed by the "Yankee Company" on the workers and peasants involved in its operations and, a few pages later, on the way its owners virtually steal Usebio's plot of land after the 1920 crash, lead the reader to assume that a major theme of the novel will be that of economic colonialism. But this is not the case. Once the plot begins to advance this element of protest practically disappears and we perceive that the real theme is the black identity and experience of Menegildo first in the countryside and then in the city. Ambiguities and inconsistencies appear in Carpentier's outlook. To some critics the beliefs and attitudes that Menegildo learns at his mother's knee and from the local witch-doctor, which lead him straight into the magic-dominated world of *ñañigo* power. (In Havana, *ñañigo* is a black brotherhood, originally of slaves, based on magic and ritual, with an initiation ceremony for new adepts like the one described in chapters 35 through 37 of *Ecue-Yamba-O*. Carpentier observed *ñañigo* ceremonies as a young man but later admitted that their real significance had been deftly concealed from him. It follows that his description of *ñañiguismo* and black rituals is at this stage hardly more than picturesque exoticism.) Such beliefs and attitudes constitute a positive alternative culture that Carpentier (implicitly for the most part) offsets against effete white Western culture. Menegildo is seen as inhabiting a somehow privileged black world, closer to nature, to belief, to human authenticity. Thus R. González Echevarría writes that "the significant thing about this novel is its fidelity to the idea of the superiority of the Black. The black world is a world governed by occult forces, in which man lives in direct communion with natural forces. In contrast the white world is a worn-out world in which man lives a mere reflected and indirect existence."[5] Certainly there is evidence of this in the text. The white world, wherever the narrative impinges upon it, is always shown as degraded and degrading. Its symbols are, as in "El milagro de Anaquillé," anachronistic posters advertising American cigarettes in the homeland of the cigar and Scott's Emulsion where sunshine and abundant fruit make it grotesquely unnecessary. Together with these go the sugar mill, which pollutes the countryside, enslaves the peasants, and emasculates the workers, the modern houses for the American staff, "smiling and with a proper air of decency like schoolgirls from a yankee college,"[6] and the top employees themselves, who enjoy whiskey and cocktails at the American hotel and behave with discreet impropriety toward their girlfriends before bringing Christmas Day to an end with drunken hymn singing.

Not all Carpentier's satire is reserved for the foreign exploiters. Another important secondary theme of the novel is the corruption of "white" politics in Cuba (e.g., the fraudulent electoral practices in which Menegildo's cousin Antonio is involved) and the equally corrupt pattern of "white" justice, seen in Menegildo's acquittal after his attack on his rival Napoleón. The fusion of this element of protest with the expression of aspects of Afro-Cuban culture is a successful feature of the novel. But, as Lloyd King argues,[7] Carpentier was careful to keep the very real political activities of the brotherhoods and their culture-preserving function artificially separate, in order to avoid contamination of the latter by the former. The fact that he mentions the brotherhoods' dubious political function at all—and at a critical point—is part of the ambiguity of his attitude to the blacks mentioned below.

Faced with the white interlopers at the mill, Menegildo "came to feel a real pride in his primitive life"(64). In contrast to the white man's religion, satirized in the reference to the "ridiculous" semigothic steeple (another anachronism) of the Company's church, the behaviour of some Jamaican salvationists and the slightly comic presentation of a Roman Catholic religious procession in chapter 37, Menegildo's absolute faith rests on "a conception of the universe which accepted the possibly magic nature of any fact"(60). On this basis he despises the ignorance the yankees reveal of the real forces governing man's existence. For him these forces belong to an occult world explained in terms of Afro-Cuban religious syncretism where Gods of African origin rub shoulders with Christ, the Virgin, and the Saints. The blacks can enter into communion with this world by means of magical ceremonies, propitiations, and rites of initiation.

By now it seems that the basic contrast of the novel is between Menegildo as a cultural hero, close to nature and to the inner mystery of things, and modern white culture, cut off from its roots. Symbols of this could be found in the cure performed by the witch-doctor when Menegildo is bitten by a poisonous crab and in the cyclone, which, in chapter 11, destroys the modern building of the whites near the mill, but allows Menegildo's family to survive, as well as in the success of Menegildo's appeal to magic in order to capture the love of Longina. But once more this is not so. The *contextos,* the specifically observed background details (in this case of *ñañiguismo*), are partly inauthentic, as Carpentier was to insist; and Menegildo's character lacks definition and his outlook and beliefs lose their validity once he leaves the rural environment for the city. As Joseph Sommers has indicated,[8] both the ironic pattern of the plot itself and the use Carpentier makes of the narrative voice undermine the notion of superior, more "natural," black values. On the one hand, as the meaning of the title suggests, Menegildo believes himself to be possessed of a deeper understanding of real reality than that enjoyed by the whites and he believes himself able to secure the help and protection of the true Afro-Cuban deities (Yemayá, Shangó, Obatalá) by means of magical rituals. On the other hand the sequence of his actions and experiences is presented as a repetitive cycle of violence and death. The novel proper really begins with Menegildo's birth and ends with the birth of his son. Its pattern is circular, and circularity in literature normally implies futility. We can, of course, take the view that Menegildo's son's life will begin at a different level from that of his father, converting the circularity into a spiral, as Carpentier was to imply rather disingenuously in the preface of the 1977 Cuban reedition of the novel. But there is no real evidence for this in the text, and Mocega-González is surely right to call it a subterfuge.[9] Menegildo appears to progress. He undergoes three successive initiations: into basic black primitive beliefs, into sexuality, and into a *ñañigo* brotherhood. But it is important to notice that the third and most important initiation, although embodied in a memorable set-piece description, is not associated with any deep spiritual response on Menegildo's part but instead leads directly to the final brawl and to his death, foretold by an omen at his birth.

It is not easy to link this convincingly with a notion of black superiority or greater "authenticity." Still less is this the case when we notice that the narrative voice in the novel is not identified consistently with Menegildo's outlook and values but slips disconcertingly into patronizing authorial comment. Nor can we overlook Menegildo's passivity with regard to the rituals, which are always presented documentally, as if observed from the outside, rather than related to the human experience and participation of the central figure. This suggests that the blacks are not really capable of understanding or expressing their own experiences. But of equal significance is the fact, so far unnoticed, that as the novel progresses Menegildo and the blacks generally tend increasingly to be presented in a grotesque and even comic light, when not in an implicitly hostile one. Thus a Negro dance in a brothel is said to take place in an atmosphere of "bestiality and voluptuousness," while the spiritualistic séances of Cristalina Valdés that Menegildo and Longina attend are surrounded by the dense effluvia of armpits, and busts of Lenin and Napoleon flank a crucifix. We notice too that the chief officiant at Menegildo's *ñañigo* initiation is revealed to be in private life a political fixer. The grotesque and the hostile unite in the description of Menegildo's entry into Havana prison, when he imagines a salvo of cannon being fired in honor of the occasion, and such crimes as his are compared to "a gesture of dangerous, animal self-affirmation."[10] We cannot, in fact, fail to notice the consistent application of animal imagery to the blacks.

Compounding these ambiguities is the style of the novel, which, apart from interludes of straight denunciation of abuses in appropriately direct language, juxtaposes avant-garde expressionist and even surrealist imagery (the latter perhaps touched up in Paris during the final rewrite) and the crude dialect of the black speakers, together with the elemental imagery through which they are presented. Nothing more clearly illustrates the ambivalence of Carpentier's approach to the Afro-Cuban world in *Ecue-Yamba-O* than this glaring and unresolved contrast. What we perceive here are not just two styles, but two linguistic codes that have both different referents and different functions. One has to do with the primitive black reality Carpentier is attempting to explore, albeit from an inescapably nonblack frame of reference. This is ever more apparent, not least in his use of non-Cuban expressions borrowed from Spanish (*rapaza, rorro* or *mozo rollizo,* for example). The other, with its vanguardist imagery, is related to the preexisting literary code, that of old-style realism, which Carpentier was attempting to subvert.

It is here, in the use of this highly intrusive, would-be innovatory second code, and in Carpentier's particular way of patterning the narrative that we can recognize the historical importance of *Ecue-Yamba-O* in the context of Cuban fiction. It is false to see in Carpentier's first novel "the old formula of *criollismo.*"[11] As he himself wrote of the attempts at stylistic innovation in the book, "the period, the tendencies . . . imposed their deformations on us, together with their verbal ecology, their crazy proliferations of metaphors, or mechanical similes, their language adjusted to the rhythms of the futurist aesthetic (for, as we can now see, that is where it all came from . . .) which, in the end, was bringing into being a new rhetoric."[12] Just as this striving for a new mode of expression contrasted with the flat, unadorned style of realism, so the arrangement of the narrative, in which incidents and descriptions are presented from different angles of vision, creates an order clearly meant to contrast with conventional linear plot development. *Ecue-Yamba-O* marks not the first, but the first really significant break with the realist/naturalist convention of novel-writing in Cuba, and it belongs to a wider pattern of change that included Enrique Serpa's timid experiments with stream-of-thought in *Contrabando* (Contraband, 1933), the "gasiform" novels of Enrique Labrador Ruiz, which began in the same year with *El labirinto de sí mismo* (The labyrinth of himself), and Lino Novás Calvo's *El negrero* (The slaver, 1933). We should notice, however, that the original draft of *Ecue-Yamba-O* preceded these other attempts at innovation.

Ecue-Yamba-O is not a fully successful novel by the standards Carpentier was later to achieve. He has said of it: "It is the work of a beginner, amusing at time, but too heavily marked by the turns of phrase and mannerisms of an outworn vanguardism—though its political attitudes, I am proud to say, were absolutely correct."[13] But it is far from being a failure or difficult to read. If we wince a little at some of the stylistic effects, standing alongside the deliberate Cubanisms, for which a glossary is provided, we enjoy the dramatic incidents and the exotic or realistic descriptions, such as those of the *ñañigo* initiation ceremony or the Havana prison conditions. It is to be regretted that Carpentier, until 1977 when he authorized a reprint, disowned the novel, which appeared at a critical moment for modern Cuban fiction and has genuine intrinsic merits.

"Histoire de lunes" (Moonstruck)[14]

On his arrival in Paris in March 1928, Carpentier was a young political exile with left-wing but as yet unformed political views. Nonetheless he immediately joined an anti-Machado political group and began propaganda work for it. In terms of his cultural development, his articles up to late 1928 suggest that he was more familiar with the avant-garde in music than in literature. At this stage, as *Ecue-Yamba-O* and the other early works show, he was an innovator in the sense that he had consciously set his face against both the themes and the techniques of the realist generation. He believed in nationalistic works, which were to be of popular inspiration (such as his own or those of his composer friend and collaborator Roldán), but also used a highly elaborate artistic mode of

expression. This had led him, as it was at the same time leading
Miguel Angel Asturias, to what has been called pleasure in the word
as sound. Examples abound in *Ecue-Yamba-O* of onomatopoeia, al-
literation, repetition of sound patterns, and balanced rhythms within
sentence construction, quite apart from the obtrusively self-con-
scious metaphors and similes. He had not yet come to believe, as
he would later, that language is not an end in itself but a means
and must be subordinated to content: "language must be adjusted
in every case to the literary composition of the novel. One must
take language as far as it will go, in accordance with the requirements
of content."[15]

Equally, around 1928, Carpentier was not yet fully aware either
of the full significance of surrealism, which, once understood, was
to be an important factor in his discovery of "the marvelous real"
or of the importance for him as a Latin American writer of a really
detailed knowledge of the past and present of his own subcontinent.
Both were to strike him forcibly almost at once. But for the moment
he brought the first phase of his work to a close with "Histoire de
lunes."

Looking backwards in the 1960s he could assert: "I thought, from
the moment I began to be really aware of what I wanted to do, that
the Latin American writer was duty bound to 'reveal' hitherto unex-
plored realities. And most of all to break away from 'nativism,'
'typicality,' picturesque set-piece descriptions, in order to 'depro-
vincialize' his literary work and raise it to the level of universal
values."[16] Paradoxically, before he could achieve this, he needed the
European experience in order to establish his full Latin American
identity. The first fruit of this experience was "Histoire de lunes,"
written (with help) in French and published in *Cahiers du Sud* at
the end of 1933, five and a half years after his arrival in Paris.

As we have seen, *Ecue-Yamba-O* contains a mixture of themes and
styles and is only partially successful in revealing the black world.
In "Histoire de lunes" on the other hand we slip imperceptibly
inside the magical Afro-Cuban outlook. The eight short parts, each
only a few paragraphs long, tell the story of Atilano, a Cuban village
bootblack and member of a black brotherhood, who, bewitched by
his "double," an eel, believes himself to be turning into a tree.
Under the influence of the spell he runs amok by night, raping the
village women. When the men join forces to hunt him down, it
turns out that he has attacked only women associated with a rival

brotherhood. His own group defend him and during the village carnival the hostilities degenerate into a riot. Atilano is arrested by the white authorities and shot on the pretext that he is a Communist agitator.

Although set roughly in the same period and the same sort of rural environment as the opening part of *Ecue-Yamba-O*, and making use of the same sort of beliefs and rituals, "Histoire de lunes" marks a great advance on the earlier novel. Here there is no ambiguity, no conflict of aims, no variations in the narrative voice, no jarring juxtapositions of styles. The story is a total unity, told with detached impersonality. The magical atmosphere is no longer picturesque and exotic; it is a living part of the mentality of the villagers, apart from the Parish priest. Hence when we move into it from the realistic opening, with its description of the arrival of the daily train to arouse the place from its lethargy, the transition is direct and unequivocal: "It was exactly at the moment when the carriages entered the station that the tree began to grow. At least what the spell caused to grow like a tree.[. . .] Suddenly he felt the seed burst in his brain, and warm roots which got progressively harder and harder came slipping along his sides. A little green snake unrolled itself along his spine to crack sharply like a whip between his thighs."[17]

Thereafter the story develops in two symmetrical phases, separated by the dramatic realization that Atilano has raped only women of the rival *ñañigo* clan. But by this time his specific activities have slipped into the background. The emphasis in the middle is firmly on the collectivity, first united by the mystery, then murderously divided. Each of the two phases is structured, with deliberate irony, not around the manhunt but around a religious event. In the first phase (chapters 3 and 4) the villagers, at the sound of ritual drums, desert the church where they are attending mass and parade with offerings to the local witch-doctor, who reveals the rapist's identity. The episode in the church is dominated by the contrast between a china dove, representing the Holy Spirit, hanging grotesquely from the ceiling on a piece of string, and the drumming, which is pointedly compared to the cooing of a monstrous pigeon. In the second phase, the rival brotherhoods mount separate religious processions, both of which are in appearance piously Catholic but are in fact superstitious and representative primarily of the mutual hatred of the rival *ñañigos*. Just as he was to do later in *El reino de este mundo*

(The Kingdom of This World), Carpentier emphasizes the triumph of magical belief over demythicized Christianity.

By shifting the story away from Atilano and toward the divisions of the entire community and the struggle between traditional Western faith and local occult belief, Carpentier has employed an alternative to the technique he had used in *Ecue-Yamba-O*. Instead of using an archetypal representative, Menegildo, to express the outlook of a larger racial group, he moves here toward what was to become one of his most persistent aspirations: to create a collective protagonist. Finally we notice that the cyclic element, already present in his first novel, appears again here. The last sentences— "Moreover people could live in peace for a few months. The evil influences of the moon were averted, for the heavenly body was entering one of the celestial triangles which neutralize its evil influence on men's brain-pans"—suggest that what has happened is no more than part of an inevitably recurring pattern of events. Bearing in mind that "Histoire de lunes" is the only document we have, apart from journalistic articles, that casts light on Carpentier's evolution as a writer between *Ecue-Yamba-O* and the middle 1940s, both its theme and technique are of great interest and give this superb little tale a place of real importance in his early creative career.

Chapter Two
Discovering "The Marvelous Real"

For about ten years after the final rewrite and publication of *Ecue-Yamba-O* and the publication of "Histoire de lunes," Carpentier seems to have produced only journalistic articles. Not until about 1943 did he start writing fiction again, but the renewed attempt was stillborn. It was to have been called *El clan disperso,* a novel about artistic life in Cuba in the 1920s, that is, in the period of Carpentier's involvement with the Grupo Minorista; but it remained unfinished. Later he thriftily used sections of it almost unchanged in *El reino de este mundo* in the 1940s, in *El siglo de las luces (Explosion in a Cathedral)* in the mid-1950s, and even in *El recurso del método (Reasons of State)* as late as the 1970s. Despite the thinness of the evidence, it is possible to obtain some glimpses of Carpentier's outlook during the decade 1933–43. There are two aspects that are important. The first is his rediscovery of his American roots. Although he was virtually bilingual and had been to school in France, it is plain that after 1928 he experienced in Paris a kind of culture-shock that awakened in him a passionate interest in the Latin America he had been forced to leave. "I felt," he recorded later, "an ardent desire to express the [Latin] American world. I still did not know how. I was attracted by the difficulty of the task because of lack of knowledge of American essences. I devoted myself for long years to reading everything I could about America, from the letters of Christopher Columbus through the Inca Garcilaso to the eighteenth century authors. For the space of eight years I don't think I did anything except read [Latin] American texts."[1]

More specifically, when we examine the journalistic articles, we perceive the immense residual influence of his musical training and interests. The preexile articles of Stravinsky, Schoenberg, and Honegger are followed by others on Maurice Jaubert and the new music, Gaillard (Carpentier's own musical collaborator), Varese as a revolutionary innovator, the Russian ballet, Villa-Lobos, Falla, Milhaud, and the avant-garde musical scene in general. It is not surprising therefore that Carpentier, the friend and collaborator of two young Cuban musicians of the time, Roldán and Caturla, eventually returned refreshed from Europe to the musical culture of his homeland and almost at once thereafter began the research on Cuban music that was to culminate in *La música en Cuba* (Music in Cuba, 1946), a book that was in turn to have a considerable spin-off in respect of his later novels.

But not all of Carpentier's serious journalism during his stay in France was concerned with music. The visual arts, the theater, and many other aspects of the cultural scene elicited from him well-informed comment. In particular one must mention painting and the surrealist movement. Carpentier's problem around the time he was preparing the final version of *Ecue-Yamba-O* was, as we can see from his article "América ante la joven literatura europea" (America facing young European literature) of June 1931 (*Crónicas*, 2:477–83), that of conciliating his already conscious desire to translate Latin America into literary terms with his anxiety to escape from the *criollista* manner of Güiraldes, Azuela, and Gallegos. So far, he had insisted on the need for Latin American works to acquire consciously artistic technique, as in "Una obra sinfónica cubana" (A Cuban symphonic work) of November 1928 (*Crónicas*, 1:39–42). But what kind of technique? And how was it to be applied? He found the answer in cubism and surrealism. In one of the first articles he sent back from Paris to *Social* he emphasizes the fact that cubism had taught us to see commonplace objects in a new light. Early in 1930 he was writing in "Pintores nuevos. Roux, el dinámico" (New painters: the dynamic Roux) (*Crónicas* 1:170): "We move in a world of prodigies. . . . The language of every good poet, on canvas, in the text, is composed of magical formulae." Alongside Roux we must set Giorgio de Chirico, whom Carpentier knew personally as well as writing about him, and about whose work the term "magical realism" had been used by the critic Massimo Bontempelli as early as 1931. De Chirico drew part of his inspiration from the realistic treatment of the unreal in the work of the Swiss German painter Boeklin (1827–1901) and from the doctrine of "surprise" in the arts of our time launched by the French poet Guillaume Apollinaire in 1917. With him we move from cubism and futurism to surrealism proper.

According to Carpentier, speaking half a century later, the *Revista de Avance* group to which he had briefly belonged in 1927 had been quite ignorant of surrealism in its best (i.e., early) phase. Once in Paris, however, the young Cuban gravitated immediately toward Breton and the surrealists and within months of his arrival had prepared an article on the movement for *Social*. It is clear that contact with surrealism marked a turning point in his literary development. He himself was to write: "Surrealism meant a great deal to me. It taught me to see 'textures,' aspects of [Latin] American life I had not noticed."[2] Such aspects were still to come, however; for the moment what contact with surrealism brought him was first of all an alternative vision of the real, a renewed awareness of "the superior reality of things" or what he had already called "marvelous reality" in "Abela en la Galería Zak" (Abela in the Zak Gallery) (*Crónicas*, 1:116), hints of which he had clearly perceived in the Afro-Cuban outlook as we see from *Ecue-Yamba-O*. Second, it brought him a greater sense of the role of faith in the magical, in the noncausal, the supernatural, as a factor in artistic creation. The impact of both discoveries is still clearly visible in the famous prologue to *El reino de este mundo* even though by the time it appeared (April 1948) he had become highly critical of surrealism itself.

The reasons for Carpentier's break with surrealism are clear enough. When he arrived in Paris the movement was already split, and he joined the anti-Breton, revisionist, and politicized faction. He watched the movement growing farther and farther away from its original inspiration toward a mechanical and systematic exploitation of surrealist gimmicks, or what he was to call in the above-mentioned prologue "the marvelous, obtained with conjuring tricks." He disapproved of its shift away from faith in a "higher reality" to "the marvelous, evoked in unbelief." Most of all he felt that he personally had nothing to contribute to surrealism as a European movement. But surrealism and Carpentier's long absence in Europe produced in him a defamiliarizing effect, so that he returned to see Latin America with fresh eyes and with full confidence in the possibility of a renewal of technique in order to express properly what he could not see. The first major results were "Viaje a la semilla" (Journey back to the source) and *El reino de este mundo*. But there is reasonable justification for guessing that before writing the first of these he produced "Oficio de tinieblas" (Morning office) and "Los fugitivos" (The fugitives).

Two Transitional Stories

While researching the history of Cuban music after his return to Cuba in 1939, Carpentier came across the statement, which he reproduced in *La música en Cuba,* that at the death of a certain General Enna in 1851 no fewer than a hundred musicians were gathered in Santiago de Cuba to perform Mozart's Requiem. It seems to have stirred him to write a story based on the implicit contrast between this example of colonial upper-class love of pomp and display and the uncontrollable forces of destruction that the tropics can unleash. The result was "Oficio de tinieblas,"[3] the title of which refers to a once-traditional form of morning service in the Roman Catholic Church for Good Friday. Müller-Bergh has argued that the form of the service itself may have influenced the structure of the tale,[4] but it should be borne in mind that direct references to the Christian religion in Carpentier's early work tend to be ironic.

The story covers a year in the history of Santiago de Cuba and tells how, after a series of premonitory events, the city is struck successively by an earthquake and a plague of cholera, but thereafter recovers quite quickly. A point of interest is the historical setting. If González Echevarría's chronology of Carpentier's work is correct, this is the first of them to be set in the colonial past, which was from then on always to fascinate its author. Another is the style, which, particularly at the beginning, still shows a residue of Carpentier's belief in the need to dress up Latin American themes with self-consciously elaborate comparisons and images. But almost at once we sense the move toward his mature "baroque" style, with its slightly archaic turns of phrase and pastichelike enumeration, the example here being the list of old musical instruments. Third, we notice, as in *El reino de este mundo* later, the contrast between the black giant Panchón with his low-life friends, and the whites. Even though they all eventually die of cholera, Panchón's group leaves behind its challenging song "Ahí va la Lola" to symbolize the spirit of the resurgent common people. The whites on the other hand are presented with a mixture of caricature and irony. Characteristic of the latter is the way death awaits the actors in a play whose title is *Entry into the Great World.*

Most of what is novel and original in "Oficio de tinieblas" is concerned with the creation of atmosphere. Here, for the first time, in combination with the historical setting, we encounter the inclusion of supernatural events that are not reported by the narratorial voice as belonging to the outlook of others, but as "real" occurrences within the story's framework of verisimilitude established by the careful references to dates, historical figures, and identifiable places. Thus suddenly we read that as Panchón left the church where the Requiem was being performed "he did not perceive that his shadow had remained behind, in the nave, painted on the stone slab on which could be read: Dust, Ashes, Nothingness."[5] Instruments, and even crockery, tinkle out on their own the death song "La sombra" and there is a mysterious reference to "The Shadows" who are responsible for the premonitory signs that precede the double catastrophe.

The story is built around three elements: the warning signs (which include Panchón's temporary loss of his shadow and culminate in the inhabitants' obsession with the ill-omened song "La sombra"); the drolly defiant song of Panchón and the common people; and the dual catastrophe, which, however, fails to still the people's song. As with the drums in "Histoire de lunes," this last intrudes into the ceremony of the mass, bringing the tale to a characteristically ironic conclusion. It is to the human spirit, not to divine protection, to which we must look for comfort in adversity. Panchón and his cronies, crushed by catastrophes utterly beyond human control, leave behind their song of unrhetorical defiance. They are already symbolic of Carpentier's confidence in man's survival through his own resources in a hostile universe.

With this, and with the mysterious signs and portents, we are not far away from *El reino de este mundo*. "Los fugitivos," however, by general consent, represents a retrogression. Although Carpentier eventually allowed it to be included in the 1970 (Barral) edition of *Guerra del tiempo (War of Time)*, he told an interviewer in the same year: "That tale, 'The Fugitives,' they keep on publishing nowadays everywhere, doesn't please me either. It belongs, in reality, to a style that isn't mine. . . ."[6] The comment is understandable. The story contains nothing that can be related to "the marvelous real." Nor does it contain any of the obvious experimentation with narrative technique that we think of in relation to, say *El acoso (Manhunt)*. Its style is direct and realistic, without intrusive archaisms or other characteristic Carpentier features. Nonetheless it is recognizably a Carpentier short story, not merely because one of the characters, don Marcial, the plantation owner, reappears in "Viaje a la semilla,"

but also because of the circularity that has already been noticed in
Ecue-Yamba-O and "Histoire de lunes" and is even implicit in "Oficio
de tinieblas." The body of the story begins with the chance meeting
of the dog from whose viewpoint the tale is told, and a runaway
slave, Cimarrón, when their friendship starts. It ends with their
second chance meeting, when the dog attacks and kills the man.
The contrast would be too mechanical if it were not intentionally
ironic. The dog, initially no less a runaway slave than the man,
does not at first attack him despite its training. Only when it has
become totally free and is living the life of pure instinct does it
finally kill (and eat) him. Yet it is not instinct that urges the dog
to kill; it is remembered training by man.

A feature of the story pointed out by González Echevarría is that
the finding of some human bones in a cave where Cimarrón and the
dog have taken refuge prefigures the scattered bones that are all
that are left of the slave at the end. What is less convincing is his
attempt to connect this episode with the sexuality that leads to
Cimarrón's recapture. The theme of the tale is visible in the contrast
between the return to natural liberty and instinct in the animal,
which largely succeeds, and the attempted return to the same in
the man, which fails. But the two are deliberately linked by the
fact that it is the memory of training in captivity that causes the
dog finally to attack the slave, who has escaped for the second time.
As in "Viaje a la semilla" and *Los pasos perdidos,* there is no possibility
of a total return to origins.

Man's inhumanity to man, apparently eluded at the beginning,
reasserts itself unexpectedly at the end. In this respect the story is
symbolic of the fact that, before 1959, in most of Carpentier's work
there is no escape. Menegildo, Atilano, Panchón, and Cimarrón all
die, like the protagonist in *El acoso* and Esteban and Sofía in *El siglo
de las luces.* But the ending is not the only interesting technical
aspect of "Los fugitivos." The story revolves round five elements:
liberty, sexuality, hunger, fear, and death. What neither Janney
nor Pérez González[7] recognizes adequately is the systematic way
Carpentier weaves these five elements into the texture of the narrative. In chapter 1, for example, they are combined with a hint of
the story's circularity, as the dog goes from the scent of Cimmarón
(who as an escaped slave symbolizes liberty), to the scent of the
bitch (sexuality), to hunger, back to the bitch, to fear, and then
back to Cimarrón. Then the spider at the end of the chapter, through

the suggestion of its web, prefigures Cimarrón's recapture (betrayed by his sexuality) and eventual death. Similarly, at first reading, we wonder why the story did not end with the natural climax of Cimarrón's death. But the coda contains the fact that the dog and its companions eat the slave's dead body. Only when we perceive the repetition of the five elements do we realize that the last chapter completes an artistic pattern.

Magical Realism and the Marvelous Real

Magical realism in fiction, reduced to its essentials, involves two elements. One of these relates to content. It concerns the selection and incorporation into an otherwise realistic narrative of events that are conventionally thought of as unrealistic, bizarre, or incredible. The other element concerns the tone and manner in which these events are introduced. This is normally quite straight-faced, so that the reader is invited to assume that they are as much parts of everyday reality as the normally observable and credible incidents that surround them. The reader is not implicitly challenged to disbelieve the account, as in a ghost story or some kinds of mystery story, which are intended to be puzzling, but is usually presented with the event as if his acceptance of it were taken for granted. The problem of magical realism derives from the type of unlikely or bizarre incidents that are selected. These can belong to different categories. The two major ones for our purpose are, first, that in which the source of the "marvelous" is explicitly and specifically Latin American, whether its roots are in the mythicolegendary and magical outlook of certain communities such as the Afro-Cubans or the American Indians, or in the endlessly astonishing history, geography, or life-styles of the subcontinent. The second major category, however, is that in which the source of the marvelous is fantasy and the creative imagination of the author, operating within a tradition that goes back to northern European romantic writers like the Brothers Grimm and Hoffmann and more recently includes figures like Kafka. A feature of this second category is that it sometimes includes important supernatural elements, presented as such, and not merely attributed to the beliefs of those involved.

This raises an issue. All magical realism demands a certain suspension of disbelief, but the degree of suspension varies greatly from writer to writer and from work to work. Carpentier's case is typical.

He does not always use magical realism in the same way or with the same implications. His basic technique is that of attributing "marvelousness" to certain aspects of the real. But a secondary technique, already present in "Oficio de tinieblas" but visible above all in "Viaje a la semilla," which for that reason occupies a unique position in his work, incorporates a genuine element of fantasy, requiring a much greater suspension of disbelief. Whether we also see *Concerto barroco* (Baroque Concierto) as belonging to this second category depends on whether we see the fantastic incidents, such as the discovery of the tomb of Stravinsky or the sight of the funeral of Wagner, as pure fantasy or as implicitly symbolic. By the same token, the subversion of conventional time is closely related to the second category.

The difference between Carpentier's two techniques is of profound importance. The first is designed to sharpen our awareness of the astonishing richness of observable reality. To the extent that such richness is attributed primarily to Latin American reality (and implicitly denied to European reality) it is a significant feature of Latin America's literary self-discovery. But the second technique, as we perceive it in "Viaje a la semilla," questions observed reality and implicitly subverts our comfortable sense of the existence of a "really real" at all. Nearly all of what has been written about magical realism in Carpentier fails to take into account this basic distinction. The best illustration of it is to be found in the contrast between *El reino de este mundo* and "Viaje a la semilla" as examples of magical realism. The former does not call for a total suspension of disbelief. It is deliberately left ambiguous whether the tide of death that sweeps across Santo Domingo in chapter 5 is due to magic, to poison alone, or to both. Similarly at the end it is intentionally left unclear whether Ti Noel is possessed of magical powers or whether what is reported to us are the ramblings of senility.[8] When on the other hand in "Viaje a la semilla" the sorcerer makes his magical passes over the ruins of the mansion and it reverts in a flash to its pre-demolition state, we are in the presence of genuine magical realism. Neither *Ecue-Yamba-O* nor "Histoire de lunes," however, belongs even to the category of the "marvelous real." For we are not required to identify ourselves consistently either with the outlook of Menegildo or of Atilano, and in neither case is their view of things presented by Carpentier as in any sense "true." In addition, the beliefs of Menegildo and Atilano are ultimately seen as negative forces, provoking rivalry, violence, and death, whereas in *El reino de este mundo* the emphasis is heavily on the positive results of the "faith" of the blacks.

Nothing is more dangerous, therefore, than to base an interpretation of Carpentier's adherence or otherwise to magical realism primarily on the prologue to *El reino de este mundo* and his later essay "Lo barroco y lo real maravilloso" (The baroque and the marvelous real).[9] In any case, as Chiampi points out,[10] even there Carpentier vacillates between a concept of the marvelous real, which in some sense alters or amplifies reality and is based on a special kind of perception, and a concept that merely reveals what is there already. The really critical question posed by "Viaje a la semilla" and possibly by certain aspects of *Concierto barroco* is whether they are based simply on the implication that reality does actually exist "out there" but is mysterious and magical, or whether (unlike Carpentier's more usual incorporation of the marvelous real into his novels) they imply any kind of skepticism about the existence of a "really real" at all.

"Viaje a la semilla"

"Viaje a la semilla" (1944), from which Carpentier has sometimes seemed to date his mature work, is a highly symbolic story, whose symbolism has not been fully explored. In it the life-story of a colonial aristocrat is told backwards from the point of his death so that everything happens in reverse. Carpentier's own comments on the tale are not specially helpful. " 'Viaje a la semilla,' " he wrote, "comes down to being a biography taken from the moment of death of the character to the moment of his birth. The game is not wholly pointless if we think that a life seen backwards or straightforward has the same characteristics at the beginning as at its end. . . . I think, in fact, that my tale 'Viaje a la semilla,' that is, Return of the Mother, prefigures future stories. Search for the mother or for the primordial element in the intellectual or telluric point of origin."[11] The second of these comments, however, with its emphasis on escape from awareness and responsibility, unites the story not only with *Los pasos perdidos* (as Carpentier goes on to acknowledge) but also, as we have just seen, with "Los fugitivos."

The house in process of demolition, which is the story's opening image, suggests the collapse of an order of existence, specifically that of its (ruined) owner, the Marquis, and of his semicolonial fellow-magnates. Similarly, as Durán indicates,[12] telling the Marquis's story backwards, beginning from his inauthenticity as a man and his financial failure, is already a definition of him as lacking in will and meaningfulness of outlook. Less specifically the destruction of the house after its owner's death may suggest a collapse of confidence in the cultural tradition upon which the older order of existence rested. Hence the implicit theme of escape and return to a paradisiacal world of "supreme liberty." But the aspiration is doomed. In the opening chapter, for instance, the acanthus-leaf decoration on the capital of a fallen pillar is said to become aware, in contact with the earth, of its nature as a vegetable, while a climbing plant is attracted to an Ionic pillar by "a family resemblance." The suggestion is that of a return to Nature foreshadowing the end, when all the materials used in the construction of the mansion, along with the ground on which it stood, return to their "original condition." But what is that original condition? It is a piece of barren ground.

Similarly don Marcial, the Marquis, unliving his life, passes through the brief phase of supreme liberty (associated with childhood and hence with naive illusion) on his way back to the womb. Here the story changes course, from the protagonist to his surroundings. But what if it had not done so? We should have continued to regress to the sperm that fertilized the egg that became the unborn Marcial and thence to his father's and mother's lives up to that point. In other words, as we find again in Los pasos perdidos, there is no primeval element, no "source," no innocent edenic existence, no "Nature" in a positive sense. Janney is wrong to posit "a state of mystical reincorporation into the universe," something "epiphanic" at the end of the tale. In human terms there is only a return to nothingness, or to an endless regression of earlier ancestors; in nonhuman terms there is only a return to bare earth.

This explains the prominence accorded to the statue of Ceres, the goddess of natural abundance. Why is she mentioned both at the beginning and end of the story, while in the middle she is seen replacing Venus? In a sense the two goddesses are symbols of time: Venus of Marcial's youth and springtime, Ceres of his autumn and maturity (and death, since she is also connected with the underworld). When we are told that the statue of Ceres is carried off by an antiquary at the end, we understand that only the historical memory of Marcial will survive. But the fate of the Ceres figure itself, as representative of nature, which is to be defaced by time and ultimately removed, also implies, like the reference to the barren ground in chapter 12, that the comforting hope of a "return to nature" is mere illusion. The search for an "essence" ends in failure.

Carpentier has suggested that among his reasons for writing the story in this way was his desire to break out of chronological linear narration. But the implications go deeper than mere literary technique. To escape from time (in Marcial's case from ruin, from old age, from solitude, to attain youth, childhood's liberty, and the security of the womb) is to escape from one of the categories in which we seek to enclose reality. Already the momentary loss of Panchón's shadow in "Oficio de tinieblas" implied a questioning of surface reality; but there it was merely a detail. If "Viaje a la semilla" was in fact written later, it is the first work by Carpentier in which he adheres deliberately to the basic presupposition of so many "new novels" in Spanish America: that reality is mysterious, ambiguous, and possibly an illusion. Hence the inexplicable "fact" that the demolition-men find the mansion totally razed to the ground the next day. Borges has written: "There is no classification of the universe which is not arbitrary and conjectural. The reason is quite simple; we do not know what the universe is."[13]

The inversion of time in "Viaje a la semilla," is not just a trick, a technical gimmick. If we accept, as Carpentier at that time, with one part of his mind, seems to have done, that "reality" in the twentieth century is no longer thought of as stable, comprehensible, or secure, and if we accept that one function of fiction is to reflect the worldview of its times, then we must expect a questioning of older, more comfortable views of reality. And how can the novelist make an exception for time, which is part of our inbuilt way of capturing and stabilizing reality? To subvert chronological time-order is to subvert the notion of a rational, intelligible world (and here we meet again the symbol at the opening of a house being demolished). The reversal of time signifies a break with everyday notions of cause and effect, notions upon which the stability of our worldview depends. Question them, and anything is possible.

But as we proceed things get more difficult, for even as the regression takes place, time still goes forward. The story begins sometime before five o'clock in the afternoon of one day and ends the following morning. This explains why, at the end of chapter 3, to Marcial it is dawn, but the clock is striking six in the evening.

When, as all critics notice, Marcial in chapter 6 has the feeling that the clocks in the house are going backwards, he is drunk. Just as when Solimán, in *El reino de este mundo,* mistakes the statue of Paulina Bonaparte for her newly dead body and begins a ritual dance to reanimate it, Carpentier here is making use of the subjective viewpoint of a character not quite fully in his right mind in order to present reality ambiguously. Marcial's drunken vision of time going backwards parallels the course taken by time in the tale as a whole, but—since we know he is drunk—it also questions it. Again, it is just possible that in chapter 3 the lawyers leave Marcial alone in his study before he greets them (i.e., in terms of the tale, they had not yet arrived and his greeting is one of welcome). But it seems more likely that things are in their normal order: he takes leave of them, after which they depart. Similarly in chapter 4 we notice that between "one afternoon" and "at dusk," there passes "all the rest of the day"; not, it would seem, in reverse. The party-scene in chapter 6 is also apparently told in normal chronological order. Thus it is not true to assume, as Mocega-González and Ramirez Molas do, [14] that the story is simply told in reverse but remains linear. In fact, it zig-zags backwards and forwards. What does this mean? It means what the ending of *Los pasos perdidos* means: that we may dream of reversing or escaping from (ongoing) time, but we must ultimately recognize that it is only a dream.

El reino de este mundo

In 1931 Carpentier had affirmed that "I hold that those countries that possess vestiges of primitive life are the most abundant in original contributions and the richest in creative potential."[15] It is clear that this awareness, already present in *Ecue-Yamba-O,* was instantly reawakened during a journey the novelist made to Haiti in 1943. The result was his second novel, *El reino de este mundo* (1949).

The famous prologue, which launched the concept of "the marvelous real of America" and was later amplified in *Tientos y diferencias* (Gropings and disagreements, 1964), reveals that by the early 1940s Carpentier had finally digested the three basic lessons that contact with surrealism had taught him in Paris. First, literature in the twentieth century must turn away from old-style realism, or what he had called in 1930 "the poor slices of life that fill bookshop windows with their pages that smell of cheap boarding houses and civil servants' dandruff,"[16] and seek the "marvelous." Second, the marvelous was not arbitrary and gratuitous but, as the prologue asserts, "an amplification of the scales and categories of reality itself"—that is to say, what he had called in his own writings on surrealism "superior reality," which became visible to those who had faith in its existence. It fulfilled an intrinsic human need for "imaginative adventure," which had been ignored by the realists. Third, there was the need for formal innovation based on conscious literary technique.

What the trip to Haiti seems to have done was to stimulate suddenly once more in Carpentier a realization that "in [Latin] America surrealism is an everyday, commonplace, habitual thing."[17] Not only, as he had half-perceived in his descriptions of *ñañiguismo* and magical beliefs in earlier works, was there to be found the marvelousness of the present, but also the marvelousness of the past, which was revealed to him in the ruins of Henri Cristophe's palace of Sans Souci and the astounding citadel of La Ferrière. Further, in Haiti above all, this marvelousness of the past was rooted in the "Faustic" presence of the Negro. "Faustic" is a word Carpentier had learned from Spengler. It meant, as he wrote in 1930, "full of longing for liberty, for the infinite and the mysterious,"[18] as distinct from "Apollonian," which implied clinging to form and exactitude. Here, then, in Haiti he had found a racial outlook that possessed "collective faith" in a wider dimension of reality than Western rationalism accepts. The blacks had in the past used that faith to nourish one of the most amazing rebellions in history and this had been followed by one of the most unlikely reigns imaginable, that of Christophe. The concept of the marvelous real matured. Almost at once Carpentier jotted down his excited impressions: "America did not need to make much effort in order to create surprising things with a terrible poetic value . . . A land of prodigies . . . Mackandall! . . . Henri Christophe!"[19] The way was opening toward what was to become part 3 of *El reino de este mundo*.

The novel, which is told from the viewpoint of a Negro slave, Ti Noel, describes panoramically the slave revolts in Haiti at the end of the eighteenth century, the Napoleonic invasion of the island and the plague that ensued, the tyranny of Christophe, and the beginning of the regime of the mulattoes. If we look carefully at its contents, we can see that up to the end of part 4, chapter 2, the predominant theme is the conflict between "the living cosmogony of the Negro,"[20] that is, the shared faith of the blacks, and the far less vigorous and meaningful outlook of the whites, divided as it is between a played-out traditionalism and the first impact of French revolutionary ideas. Once the original conflict has been decided in favor of the mulattoes (not the blacks as such), the emphasis shifts to the wider question of the dynamics of human progress in general. It is with regard to this concluding section that the main critical disagreement exists.

The body of the book, then, develops the contrast between native beliefs and white, one that was symbolized by the sound of the *ñañigo* drums breaking into the celebration of the mass in "Histoire de lunes." The structure of the opening chapter is very relevant here. Every exposition in a play or a novel should fulfill at least four functions. It must grasp the reader's interest; it must convey enough background information for us to understand the plot; it must introduce one or more of the major characters; and finally, it should normally announce or imply the theme. Carpentier's insistence on technical proficiency, so often reiterated in his articles of the 1930s, had by now borne fruit. In contrast to the space-dominated, accretive descriptivism of the opening of *Ecue-Yamba-O,* here as in the rest of the novel everything is replaced by symbolism.

The opening symbol is that of the horses, which, as any reader of Lorca will recognize, stand for virility. Ti Noel, the slave, rides a fine stallion, while his French master, Lenormand de Mazy, rides a more delicate sorrel. The contrast establishes economically the difference between the effete white landowner (who in three marriages has no children) and the vitality of the black, who sires twelve on a kitchen maid. This initial contrast is later reinforced by the comparison of the bewigged and powdered heads (i.e., the land-owners) in the barber-shop window with the skinned, bloodless calves' heads at the butcher's, ready for consumption. Next the contrast is extended in Ti Noel's mind to one between the effeminate kings of Europe in their ballrooms and the "real" kings of Africa, charging at the head of their armies. The pattern culminates at the end of the chapter in an implicit contrast between the "real" Gods and the "real" heaven of Africa and those of the whites. The two figures on horseback of the first paragraph have led us toward a potential conflict of two races and two religions.

We are in French Haiti in the middle eighteenth century (historically, 1752). Ti Noel has heard of the kings and gods of Africa—that is, he has learned the myths that will power the future rebellion—from a fellow slave, Mackandal, who is suddenly introduced, without further description, as his mentor. Thus we are prepared for the story of the two successive slave uprisings, which seem by the end of part 2 to conclude with the triumph of the black god of war, Ogún Badagrí. After the initial chapter, the rest of part 1, and the first four chapters of part 2 chronicle the two rebellions. In the first, under Mackandal himself, a secret organization of blacks uses poison both on animals and on whites to terrorize the latter and find liberation. The attempt fails and Mackandal is forced to go into hiding, but not before he has been acclaimed a *haugán,* a miracle-working representative of the black divinities, charged with exterminating the whites and freeing the slaves. For four years the latter build up their faith in his magical power to transform himself into animals, insects, or birds. When he reappears (significantly at Christmas) and is captured, they still believe him to be invulnerable. Their faith is rewarded when he appears to break his bonds and escape from being burned alive at the stake. He is in fact thrust back into the fire, but to the blacks the African gods have miraculously saved him. Ti Noel celebrates symbolically by impregnating his slave wife so that she bears twins. His master, by contrast, makes speeches in bed to his frigid, ultra-Catholic second wife.

The second rebellion, headed by Bouckman, twenty years later (historically forty years had passed), marks an advance on Mackandal's. This time the blacks have achieved a certain political consciousness. They are vaguely aware of the *Declaration of the Rights of Man,* published by the revolutionaries in France in 1791. They rise in armed rebellion and (still convinced of the support of the African deities) loot the haciendas and rape the white women. This second, collective and more organized uprising is also crushed and followed by a fierce repression, but this time Lenormand and other white landowners are forced to flee to Cuba.

So far the plot has been linear, chronological, and limited to the area of Lenormand's hacienda and the nearby city. Now it shifts to Cuba and then to the visit to Haiti by Paulina Bonaparte with her husband, General Leclerc, commissioned by the French government to suppress the blacks. We learn of the flight of Paulina to Tortuga and of the death of Leclerc from the plague. Her subsequent return to Europe is followed by the total moral collapse of the white settler class on the island. What are the functions of this interlude? One of the features of the plot is its striking compactness and dramatic rapidity of tempo, produced by rigorous selection of episodes, brusque leaps forward in time, and deliberate suppression of descriptive presentation of character. Each of the two revolts is compressed into two chapters; Mackandal and Bouckman appear in the text without introduction and we know nothing of them personally; four years flash past at the end of part 1, chapter 6, and twenty more between part 1 and part 2. The whole technique is spare and taut, almost schematic, with large areas of background simply left out so as to emphasize the successive confrontations between the black deities and their followers and the white deity and power structure, in which it is the latter that are defeated.

As the interlude begins, the first phase of the book, that of the rebellion, is over. The second phase, that of black power (first of Christophe, then of the mulattoes), is still to come. Historically, in between, there occurred the years of the struggle of Toussaint L'Ouverture against Leclerc, the regime of Dessalines, and the early years of Christophe. But these are not to Carpentier's purpose, for voodoo was less relevant to them. What he wants to show is an ironic contrast between the struggles of Mackandal and Bouckman on the one hand and the peak of Christophe's tyranny on the other. The interlude of Paulina acts as a hinge between the two halves of the book, concealing the historical gap. At the same time it points forward to the contamination of Christophe as a black ruler by Napoleonic imperial grandiosity. But, most importantly, it rams home yet again two features of Carpentier's approach. First there is the moral degeneracy of the whites, which we saw implicitly ascribed by Menegildo to the yankees in chapter 15 of *Ecue-Yamba-O*. Lenormand, along with his second and third wives, is deliberately caricatured from the moment the former leaves the barber-shop, his cheeks caked with powder and smiling "stupidly," to the point at which he abandons his masonic beliefs and whines his repentance in the Cathedral of Santiago de Cuba before disappearing from the novel as suddenly as he had been called into it. Paulina's frivolity, sensuality, luxury, and cowardice when the plague strikes, followed by her renewed self-indulgence while escorting her husband's body home to France, climax Carpentier's presentation of white decadence in contrast to the virility and vitality of the blacks. We have seen that this decadence is founded on decay of belief. This is the second ideological feature of Paulina's presentation. The scene in which she precipitately rejects the unbelief in which she had been brought up, only to plunge into a world of magic and superstition conjured up by her voodoo-practicing black masseur Solimán, parallels with even heavier irony the apostasy from Masonry of Lenormand. Black faith and black vitality overcome even a sophisticated European princess.

The first chapter of part 3 reaffirms their triumph. Ti Noel returns from Cuba around 1820 to a land in which slavery had apparently been abolished forever. He knows and gives thanks for the fact that the gods of black Africa had intervened on the side of the slaves. But their triumph is ironic, for as Ti Noel passes Mackandal's former hideout, he is venturing into the realm of a tyrant, Christophe, who is far more oppressive than the French settlers had ever been and, what is worse, black. But the ideological thrust of parts 1 and 2 survives. For Christophe is not ruling in the name of the black African deities. He too has backslid. Rejecting the Africanist mystique of the first leaders of Haitian independence, he has allowed the Virgin and Roman Catholic saints to usurp their places. His priests are those of a parody of Christianity, which, at the last, betrays his trust. The drums of the "true" Gods announce his downfall.

Part 4 begins with a second interlude, this time in Rome in the early 1820s, where Christophe's former queen and surviving daughters are living attended by Solimán. In one respect this interlude completes the pattern of part 3. It is intended to emphasize the speed with which a privileged group or class decays when its power has been lost. At the same time the picture of the degraded reality of Rome, the center of Catholicism and one of the cradles of European civilization, reemphasizes the dubious value of European influence (whether progressive, as in the case of the French revolutionary doctrines, or as here traditional) on Latin America. The theme recurs in *Los pasos perdidos* and *El recurso del método*. In another respect, the encounter of Solimán with the Canova statue of Paulina Bonaparte, in which he drunkenly mistakes it for her corpse and tries to resuscitate it by a magic ritual, followed by his death invoking Papa Legba, the god of travel, is designed to dramatize the transmission of voodoo to the Eternal City itself and thus to underline afresh the coexistence of the two religious and cultural systems present in the novel.

The collapse of Christophe's rule is the prelude to a parody of it as Ti Noel, now senile, enjoys a brief "rule" at the former Lenormand hacienda. We notice that he uses the French *Grande Encyclopédie,* the source of so much revolutionary utopian thought, merely to sit on and that he welcomes to his court, where every day is a holiday and Ti Noel's commands merely babblings, priests of the black Church. Thus he avoids all the errors of Christophe: oppression, Europeanization, and the rejection of local beliefs. But the brief idyll is designed to contrast with the return of oppression under the mulatto regime of Boyer, in which forced labor takes the place of earlier slavery. White oppression, followed by black tyranny, has ended in mulatto coercion.

We now come to the much-debated ending in which Ti Noel "transforms" himself into a series of symbolic creatures: a bird, naturally free and able to look down on the human condition, but irrelevant to it; a stallion, powerful and vital, but subject to castration and enslavement by a mulatto; a bee or an ant, endlessly laboring and finally dying; and lastly a goose, seeking unsuccessfully to join a closed, aristocratic caste, orderly (in contrast to the disorder of social upheaval) but selfish. All of these signify possible options for man involved in historical change: to stand outside, to submit, to exist passively, to seek the protection of some powerful group. But all involve some degree of abrogation of responsibility. Ultimately Ti Noel, like Esteban in chapter 34 of *El siglo de las luces,* is invaded by a sense of "cosmic weariness" when faced by the spectacle of "the uselessness of all rebellion" and the apparently endless recurrence of oppression. But it is attended by a moment of supreme lucidity in which he achieves a double recognition: first, that man's destiny must be fulfilled here below and not in any possible heaven; second, that man's destiny on earth is to suffer, labor, and wait, struggling on behalf of a future generation, which in its turn will struggle to improve the lot of its successor, and so on forever. "But the grandeur of man lies precisely in the will to improve the existing state of affairs. To impose Tasks on himself" (p. 156). Ti Noel, as an archetypal man caught up in the eternal struggle, is, as his name Petit Noel and the title of the last chapter, "Agnus Dei," suggest, a kind of Son of Man, like the hero of the Paraguayan Augusto Roa Bastos's novel of that name. His role is to suffer and sacrifice himself for his brothers on this earth, not to redeem them for a reward in heaven.

Ramírez Molas[21] points out that this passage can be compared to Esteban's recognition in *El siglo de las luces* that "there is no other Promised Land than that which man can find within himself" and comments that this could well be the substance of Carpentier's humanistic creed. But there are problems. At this stage of his work, Carpentier's outlook is both ambiguous and ironic. There are several important instances of irony in *El reino de este mundo*. We notice, for instance, that the black king who seems in chapter 1 to stand for "true" monarchy in fact portends the rise of Henri Christophe. We cannot overlook the fact that Mackandal is in fact put to death and that the slaves' faith in his reappearance is an illusion. Third, the great cyclone that Ti Noel foresees in part 1, chapter 6, which was to be unleashed by the African gods to complete the work of men's hands—that is, to complete the liberation of the slaves—in fact appears as the last event of the novel and merely seems to coincide with, or perhaps produce, Ti Noel's death. At a deeper level, there are recurrent references in Carpentier's work, before its last phase, to the theater. Their cumulative effect seems at times to suggest that the struggle and suffering of man are no more than a fictional spectacle for the reader to contemplate. If such a distancing mechanism is in fact present, it provides a useful argument for those critics who wish to distinguish between Carpentier's earlier and later ideological outlook.

Technically the predominant feature of *El reino de este mundo* is the extreme compression and consequent speed of the narrative, achieved by large-scale elimination both of physical description and psychological commentary. There is nothing to compare with the descriptions in *Ecue-Yamba-O*, spread over several chapters, of the hurricane or the *ñañigo* initiation ceremony. One might compare for example the three-page presentation of Bouckman's magical ceremony before his rebellion or the way both Bouckman and Mackandal are presented directly through their beliefs and actions, without any conventional character buildup. The only major piece of description is that of Sans Souci and La Ferrière, but this is highly functional within the presentation of Christophe's tyrannous regime. The result is an essentially "scenic" technique in which the interpretation of events is suggested not by authorial intervention or by manipulation of the characters' words or thoughts, but by the cyclic sequence of the events themselves. This is what the British novelist J. B. Priestley meant when, in the introduction to the (New York) 1967 trans-

lation of the novel, he distinguished between "symbols stuck into
the narrative like plums into a cake" and "symbolic action, which
demands that every setting, every important event . . . have symbolic depth and value."

Supporting symbolism and the ironic arrangement of certain episodes have already been mentioned. Another important feature of
this "novel without a central character," as Carpentier called it,[22]
is the elimination of the hero and consequentially of love-interest
as such, though sexuality, as we saw, plays an important role in
distinguishing Ti Noel from the degenerate whites. The role of Ti
Noel, whose close-up view of events alternates with that of a more
distant and omniscient narrator, and who emerges into the forefront
of events in the second half of the novel, is highly interesting. We
are much closer to him as a human being than we were to Menegildo
in *Ecue-Yamba-O*. But the main difference is that Menegildo sees
voodoo from the outside, while Ti Noel, as both Barreda Tomás
and Rodríguez Monegal[23] have noticed, is completely involved in
it and thus allows Carpentier to present certain "magical" events as
if they were factual. Others (such as the appearance of the ghost of
Breille to Christophe or Ti Noel's various metamorphoses at the
end) are described more ambiguously; only one is shown specifically
in a European perspective as a collective myth (the supposed escape
from burning of Mackandal). The overall aim here is to reinforce
the implicit interpretation of the historical process followed out in
the novel, that is, to stress the importance of black supernatural
beliefs as a force to be reckoned with in the achievement of revolutionary social change.

The overriding effect is one of extreme functionality of the narrative units within the design of the work as a whole. In Barthesian
terms there is a high concentration of "cardinal narrative functions"
relative to those in which the action does not noticeably progress.
Similarly there is a predominance of "characterizing signs" over
those that are merely randomly informative in a realistic sense.

Chapter Three
Time and Circularity
"Semejante a la noche"

Emil Volek[1] records that Carpentier in 1966 told him categorically that "Semejante a la noche" (Like the night), first published, as was "Oficio de tinieblas," in the Cuban magazine *Orígenes,*[2] was written in 1947. He goes on to assert that it is therefore to be considered an earlier effort than *El reino de este mundo* (1949). The assertion rests on the assumption that the latter novel was written shortly before its publication. But Carlos Rincón has reproduced a version of what was to become part 3, chapters 2 through 7 of *El reino de este mundo,* taken from materials originally intended for Carpentier's *El clan disperso.*[3] This first draft was published as early as May 1944. It reveals how carefully we must treat the dating of Carpentier's works. The author himself has specifically stated that he interrupted the writing of *El reino de este mundo* in order to visit Mexico in 1944. It follows that if Rincón is correct in giving 1946–47 as the time of the main writing of the novel in question, Carpentier was probably writing it along with *La música en Cuba,* which was commissioned in 1944 and published in 1946. Moreover the first published version of "Semejante a la noche" carried a by-line dating it September 1949, doubtless referring to a final revision, perhaps while *El reino de este mundo* was in press. We must therefore conclude that the three works were roughly contemporaneous, *El reino de este mundo* having been begun before *La música en Cuba* and "Semejante a la noche" having been finished last.

To a greater or lesser extent, "Semejante a la noche" and certain other stories in *Guerra del tiempo* present a problem to those who wish to see Carpentier's attitude to time and historical progress in a positive light. For a common theme of the collection is ironic repetition, which can readily be interpreted as a negation of progress. Statements by Carpentier himself can be and have been used to support such an interpretation. His remarks to César Leante, for instance: "Man is at times the same in different ages and to situate him in his past can also be to situate him in his present"[4] and to Claude Fell (à propos of "Semejante a la noche" itself): "I think that man has a single pattern of behavior amid changing circumstances. That is what I showed in the tale in *Guerra del tiempo* entitled 'Semejante a la noche,' "[5] seem at first sight to admit no argument. But the former closely follows Carpentier's definition of the theme of *El siglo de las luces*: "Men can weaken, but ideas make their own way and in the end find their application,"[6] which seems to imply that he himself saw no contradiction between the postulate of man's unchanging nature and that of historical progress. In fact it becomes clear in his later work that he saw man's unchanging nature, insofar as it exists, as an individual phenomenon, while progress is a collective one. We notice that, as elsewhere in Carpentier's thought, the fit with a mainline Marxist outlook is somewhat awkward.

"Semejante a la noche" deals with a series of departures in which a young man goes forth to war. Its theme is man's endless tendency to embark on warlike expeditions with the illusion that the conflict will be justified at the collective level by the righteousness of the cause and the expansion of national power, and at the individual level by the superiority of the profession of arms and the prestige and social advantages it brings. The actual departure produces a certain disillusionment as the young soldier realizes that the glamour of war is the result partly of propaganda and partly of self-deception. The reality is the conquest of economic advantage for others by common soldiers who share the danger but not the privileges of the officer class. Nonetheless the enterprise goes on.

The story illustrates the way in which a commonplace, creaky, oversimplified idea can coexist with brilliant technical originality. For what matters here is not the tale's obtrusive didacticism, but the way in which Carpentier fuses together preparations for five different expeditions into a single allegorical whole. We begin with a young Achaean footsoldier about to set out with Agamemnon's fleet for Troy. But this departure dissolves into that of a young Spaniard about to start in the sixteenth century for the ongoing conquest of the New World. In turn it becomes that of a young French adventurer in the seventeenth century bound for the Gulf of Mexico. But now, hardly noticed (especially by certain critics), we move for an instant back to the twelfth century and the beginning of a Crusade, before moving on to our own times and a young North American soldier on the point of setting out for the invasion of

France in World War II. González Echevarría's view that this scene refers to World War I[7] and therefore that there are six time-notations is rendered doubtful by the fact that aluminum aircraft wings did not become common until the 1930s.

As the temporal shifts succeed one another, the story is held tightly together not only by the central figure, who is implicitly the same first-person narrator at every stage, but also by other devices. First, another series of time-notations indicates successively dawn, morning, afternoon, evening, a few hours before dawn, and finally dawn once more. Thus the shifts over almost three thousand years occur within the space of one symbolic "day." While, that is, the single narrator stands for man's unchanging nature, the juxta-position of millennia and a single day and the circularity of the time-notations suggest the possibility that time itself is an illusion. Second, a carefully graduated interplay of repetitions and develop-ments emerges as the story progresses. The problem facing Car-pentier was that of balancing the two, so that the repetition would not become mechanical. Hence in the first two episodes the final emphasis is on the young soldier's relationship with his parents, who, though apprehensive, are placated in the second by an appeal to religious justification and family pride. In the third episode the pattern changes to that of the young man's relationship with his unofficial fiancée. This is linked to the previous sequence by the uneasiness of both mother and fiancée at the presumed nakedness of the native women in the New World. But it is differentiated not only by the shift in emotional allegiance, for the younger woman rejects the religious justification that the mother had accepted. The discussion is inconclusive. But the brief mention of a Crusade, which the young man declines to join, indicates with gentle irony the insincerity of his professions of higher motives. Hence the posi-tioning of the tiny episode at this strategic point. For this reason, and in view of the shift away from religion toward sexuality in the latter part of the story, Assardo's interpretation of it in terms of religious symbolism[8] must be treated with the same caution as Maturo's cognate interpretation of *Ecue-Yamba-O* and *El reino de este mundo*.[9]

The young man's twentieth-century girlfriend is linked to the earlier girl and to the mother by contrast. Unlike them, she appears neither apprehensive nor hostile. She seems to accept spontaneously and even enthusiastically her companion's now unspoken self-justification, and this time any nakedness is on her part. Is it perhaps relevant that the young soldier is now about to fight Nazism? In any event, the pattern so far is reluctant endorsement (followed by mass); rejection (followed by flight and frustration); total endorsement (followed by sexual fulfillment). It is this rising and falling pattern of parallelism between the soldier's justification and the response of others close to him that governs the structure of the tale, as distinct from its symbolic meaning. To provide the end-situation, the pattern is abruptly reversed, yet not entirely broken. From the opening page, references to sexuality have been present. After the implicit rejection of the crusade-myth in part 4 these displace the religious motif, which thereafter completely disappears, and culminate in the nakedness of the twentieth-century woman. Sexuality replaces the mass as a sign of endorsement. At the end of the tale this response is offered afresh, but without any previous discussion of justification. But the soldier is too exhausted by love-making earlier in the night and initiates the series of ironies that conclude the story by failing to accept the girl's offer of her virginity. What she had jealously feared would happen in the Indies does not happen at home when the opportunity arises! But there is more than this. The illicit act of love that the young man is unwilling to risk with his fiancée is the same act that provides the pretext for the war. He is unable to enjoy his Helen but is about to risk his life for a Helen who is enjoying herself to the full. This less obtrusive irony should not be concealed by the much more obvious, and cruder, one of the underlying economic motive for the war, which at length jars with the soldier's professions of idealism.

"El camino de Santiago"

The very close thematic relationship between "Semejante a la noche" and "El camino de Santiago" (The highroad of St. James) makes it appropriate to deal with the latter at this point. The first two chapters were published in the newspaper *El Nacional* of Caracas in 1954 along with mention of the fact that the whole story had been accepted for publication. But in the view of González Echevarría a first draft may have been begun as early as 1947. [10] Carpentier has implied that its actual writing overlapped with that of *Los pasos perdidos* and *El acoso*. The stimulus seems to have come from the discovery of a reference to a certain Juan de Emberes, who played the drum in Cuba in 1557, which Carpentier made while researching *La música en Cuba.*

The tale is that of Juan de Amberes, a picaresque figure, who at the beginning is a drummer in the Spanish army in sixteenth-century Flanders. Terrified by an outbreak of plague, he begins a pilgrimage to Compostela but is persuaded to abandon it in order to emigrate to Cuba. There he knifes an adversary in a fight and has to flee to the outback, where he shares the lives of a Jew and a Calvinist along with some blacks. At length, homesick, he manages to return to Spain and there persuades another pilgrim to return with him to the Indies. Doubts on the part of the Virgin Mary about his spiritual suitability as a settler are overcome by St. James, who wishes to see Spanish civilization spread, even by such ruffians.

A critical problem of "Semejante a la noche" was that it seemed to suggest the futility of the various warlike expeditions that are mentioned and even to imply a static, circular vision of time. But the liberation of Europe from Nazi occupation could hardly be regarded as a futile exercise, and this gives pause for thought. Equally, the conquest and settlement of America, to which the second and third expeditions in "Semejante a la noche" relate, can be seen in a different light from that which the last paragraph of the story appears to suggest, if we take into account the ending of "El camino de Santiago." There St. James is heard interceding with the Virgin on behalf of the two Juans and their follower Golomán, on the grounds that even expeditions composed of "such knaves" will in the end produce the founding of a hundred new cities.

An obvious way of reading "El camino de Santiago," then, is to relate it backwards through "Semejante a la noche" to the ending of *El reino de este mundo* and forward to the ending of *El siglo de las luces.* This is in fact the reading proposed by Rodríguez-Alcalá and developed by Dorfman.[11] The deception practiced on Juan the Pilgrim when he is diverted from his pilgrimage to Compostela by the picture of America drawn by Juan of the Indies, and the same deception, which he in turn practices on another pilgrim after returning to Spain, correspond to the myths that powered the black rebellions in Haiti and the myth of the Promised Land, seen by Esteban in *El siglo de las luces* as symbolic of mankind's ongoing journey through history. Man needs such myths in order to act and influence the course of events. Even if they are false, even if the outcome is at first sight disappointing, something will have changed.

From the infinitesimally slow changes comes onward progress. "Sisyphus changes history," Dorfman writes. "It seems to be the same stone, but it is not. It seems to be the same mountain, but it is not. To get rid of the stone Sisyphus seeks another reality, of airy illusion, only to find himself again, in the fullness of time, with the same burden. But it is not the same one. This is one of Carpentier's fundamental messages."[12]

In view of the great divergence of critical opinion about Carpentier's attitude to time and progress, this can be seen as suggesting only one approach to "El camino de Santiago." Other critics have seen the story as a religious allegory of man's "spiritual decaying and downfall,"[13] due to his surrender to sin and the worldly illusion of liberty and a terrestrial paradise, instead of repenting and seeking heaven. In terms of this interpretation, the vital incidents in the story are Juan's abandonment of his pilgrimage and the murder he commits in the New World, which confirms and accelerates his moral collapse. It is difficult to incorporate into this approach either the heavy emphasis on religious fanaticism and cruelty or the final episode, in which the two Juans are seen by the Virgin and St. James, not as sinners but as men whose moral shortcomings are less important than their role as potential founders of new communities in the Indies. It does seem as if Saint and Virgin are made tacitly to endorse Carpentier's dictum that individual salvation is to be worked out here below, through participation in a collective historical enterprise. Nonetheless, in view of the strong current of critical interest in the religious aspects of Carpentier's work, which surface again in *El acoso* and "Los advertidos" (The chosen), this approach to "El camino de Santiago" merits careful attention.

The details of the story illustrate González Echevarría's view that the research for *La música en Cuba* provided Carpentier with a new creative pattern, that of historical pastiche, with elements selected from documental and historical sources. There are clear references in the tale both to *Os Lusíadas* and *Lazarillo de Tormes,* and the whole work is close to the picaresque genre. Some names and details can be traced to historical documents, and the events can be dated to some extent around the year 1568. It is questionable, however, whether this in any way affects the interest or meaning of the tale. More questionable still is the point borrowed by Magnarelli from González Echevarría that the reflection of earlier literary works should incline us to see the tales referent as literature alone, and not "reality" or human experience. Extraliterary factors cannot thus be blithely ignored.

Once more we are in the presence of deliberate craftsmanship. We see again how the opening is full of portents of the rest: the two drums, which prefigure the two Juans; the references to cards and brandy, which introduce the theme of Juan's surrender to the flesh; the mistiness, pointing to Juan's befogged outlook before his realization at the end of chapter 2, which is accompanied by a clear sky and a bright Milky Way; the oranges connected with the Duke of Alba's mistress, suggestive of fleshly delights in a hot climate. Chapters 2 through 4 are linear and comparatively unambiguous, dealing with Juan's dream, guilt feelings, vow, and eventual backsliding, marked at the end of the section by the return of mist to hide the Milky Way, which stands for the road to Compostela and heavenly salvation. The Milky Way salvation symbol reappears during Juan's feverish nightmare in Cuba and finally in the last line of the tale, after he appears to have been forgiven by the Virgin, as if to reaffirm that he is to be granted salvation in return for his participation in the conquest and settlement of the Indies. If, of course, the theme of the story is man's corruption, the final reference must be seen as ironic.

In the center of the tale, chapters 5 through 8, the rhythm changes. The narration becomes slower and more charged with Carpentier's characteristic, enumerative descriptions. The emphasis, too, changes. The main line of the tale (Juan's evolution) continues. After the affray in Havana has added anger and violence to his carnal backsliding, the "night" that descends on him as his hat is pulled over his eyes symbolizes deeper spiritual darkness. Before long, pride—the sin of Satan himself—is added as Juan boasts of his pretended lineage and studies. But meanwhile the story has bifurcated. Juan, the fanatical burner of Lutherans, is now living and even praying alongside a Calvinist, a Jew, and some pagan natives. But on returning to the Old World the Calvinist and the Jew are ill-treated by the Catholics and handed over to the Inquisition. These two new characters and the theme they represent, tolerance as against intolerant cruelty, seem to have no direct connection with either of the two interpretations of the tale mentioned above. What are they there for? Especially, what is the function of chapter 9, in which Juan is no more than an apprehensive onlooker? These characters and episodes lend ambiguity to a story that, like most semi-allegorical tales, would otherwise be rather schematic and simplistic. America does not live up to the first settlers' description of it, except in one respect: there is greater religious freedom. Second, while it is true that Juan fails to live up to the religious obligations he has assumed, the Calvinist and the Jew are there to remind us—why else should Carpentier have introduced them, and not others?—that the religion in question is cruel and fanatical.

The last section of the story, chapters 10 and 11, reduplicates the situation of chapters 4 and 5 in order to symbolize the repetitive nature of man's tendency to follow terrestrial illusions rather than the promptings of his spiritual nature. Since the latter appear to include oppressing and burning one's fellow men, while the former lead to the incorporation of Latin America into a process that, though terribly slow and irregular, is ultimately one of human progress, we can understand the endorsement of St. James and the final symbolic brightness of the Milky Way. Carpentier's comment, included in a note to the 1954 Caracas fragment of the story: "It should be noticed, however, that as the story progresses, Juan de Amberes gradually changes into a character who could well be a contemporary of ours,"[14] seems to suggest that a purely religious interpretation of the story, as if it were a seventeenth-century morality tale (as, for instance, Verzasconi seems to view it), is less plausible than one that is in line with the conclusion of *El reino de este mundo.*

Chapter Four
A Journey through Time
The Background to *Los pasos perdidos*

When Carpentier returned to Cuba from Europe in 1939, a major phase of his life came to a close; but a new and far more productive one was about to begin. The decision to return to his native island must have been a difficult one. He was now in his late thirties and had spent a large part of his early manhood in France. His parents having been immigrants to Cuba, he had no extensive family ties or deep roots to pick up. In Paris he had combined a successful and adequately paid career in broadcasting with journalism, which had made him a kind of cultural outpost of Havana in the French capital. He had a wide circle of friends in Europe and had remained politically active, joining a fellow Cuban, the poet Nicolás Guillén, as well as Malraux, Octavio Paz, Neruda, Vallejo, Langston Hughes, and others in a distinguished delegation to the Second Congress of Writers in Defense of Culture in Republican Madrid in 1937.

By 1939, however, he had become disillusioned with Europe. War was clearly imminent, a war with which Carpentier does not seem to have felt involved. Europe appeared bankrupt of spiritual values. It looked as though Spengler, in *The Decline of the West,* had been right after all. A visit to Cuba in 1936 had intensified Carpentier's nostalgia and now he returned definitively to the New World. But to start afresh was not easy. He was virtually unknown as a writer and his journalism did not produce enough to make ends meet, especially after his marriage to Lilia Esteban. He was forced onto a treadmill of writing, producing and directing ephemeral radio programs, and giving classes in musicology at the Conservatory. The war had broken links with Europe, without as yet revealing the stimulating effect that this was to have in the long run on New World culture. Carpentier must have felt marginalized. In the early 1940s his most important writings were a series of articles for *Carteles* ("El ocaso de Europa" [The dusk of Europe]), not since republished, on the imminent demise of the Old Continent. They reveal a strong

confidence in the young culture of the New World and rejection of
European art (especially surrealism), which reappear in the prologue
to *El reino de este mundo,* first published as an article in *El Nacional*
of Caracas on 4 April 1948.

Meanwhile two factors of major importance for his future work
supervened. The first was his research into Cuban musical history,
which began soon after his return. It seems to have antedated his
commission in 1944 to write *La música en Cuba,* published two years
later. The orientation toward the past and toward documentation
that went with the work have been seen as presenting him with a
new approach to his fiction. Henceforth the element of historical
pastiche was to remain prominent right up to *El arpa y la sombra*
(The harp and the shadow; 1979). The second factor was fortuitous.
The famous French actor Louis Jouvet, whom Carpentier had got
to know in Paris, arrived in Cuba in late 1943 and invited him and
his wife to go to Haiti. There Carpentier was able to visit the ruins
of Henri Cristophe's palace and fortress and to see the house of
Paulina Bonaparte. The impact on him was immediate. Abandoning
his half-finished novel, *El clan disperso,* set in Cuba in the late 1920s
and early 1930s and dealing with the activities of the Grupo Minorista and the fall of Machado, he began at once *El reino de este
mundo.* But before he had got very far, he accepted during a holiday
in Mexico the commission for *La música en Cuba.* Work on this for
the moment became his main writing. But as the book neared
completion in mid-1945, Carpentier's life took a new turn. A friend
from Parisian days, Carlos Frías, invited him to join a new broadcasting and advertising venture in Caracas. The prospect of a more
stable income with less fragmentation of effort seems to have decided
Carpentier to accept. He was to remain in Caracas, where he became
a regular contributor to the daily paper *El Nacional,* until the triumph
of Castro in 1959.

By that time he had published thousands of short articles in the
paper, most of which remain uncollected. By far the most important
are the series "Visión de América" (A vision of America), four of
which appeared in *El Nacional* between 19 October and 7 December
1947, to be later republished in Havana along with a fifth about
Ciudad Bolívar. The articles, which can be found in volume 2 of
his *Crónicas,* describe a trip by air from the latter city on the Orinoco
in July 1947 to the almost unknown interior of southeastern Venezuela. The following year Carpentier made another trip, this time

westward to the Upper Orinoco by bus and launch. Initially it had been his intention to write a nonfictional account of his first journey, to be called *El libro de la Gran Sabana* (The book of the Great Savannah), but, like *El clan disperso,* this book never came to completion. It was overtaken by the inspiration for a new novel in which Carpentier combined the impressions of his launch journey and his flight, involving two quite different parts of Venezuela, to provide the setting for *Los pasos perdidos.* "And I recall that one extraordinary, brilliant evening," he wrote, "I had something like an illumination: the novel *Los pasos perdidos* was born in a few seconds, completely structured, ready-made. . . ."[1] Clearly what Carpentier's two forays into the interior of Venezuela provided him with was in the first place a staggeringly impressive background, which not only suited his taste for set-piece descriptions, but could also be adapted to fit in with part of the meaning of the novel: the discovery of a region of timeless and mysterious features that could be associated with the dream of ultimate happiness, the finding of El Dorado. But it was not just the scenery. In addition Carpentier's journeys brought him into contact with white jungle dwellers, notably the source-figures for El Adelantado and Fray Pedro, men who seemed to have escaped from the fears and stresses of modern life and to have found Utopia.

Los pasos perdidos

In *Los pasos perdidos* an unnamed narrator, by profession a composer, tells retrospectively how he allowed himself to be persuaded by his mistress, Mouche, to leave for a while his unsatisfying marriage and escape from the New York rat-race. On the pretext of searching for primitive musical instruments, the couple embark on an expedition to the Amazonian jungle. Once there, their relationship collapses as the narrator finds not only the instruments, but also self-fulfillment with a new companion, Rosario, in a primitive settlement. The narrator recovers both his physical and spiritual balance and at the same time his creativity. But the resources of the settlement do not allow him to compose. He returns to New York determined to liquidate his marriage and escape again to the jungle with all he needs. But he is unable to find his way back and is relentlessly drawn again into his former life-style.

Several critics have commented on the lack of psychological depth in Carpentier's characters.[2] Carpentier himself has spoken of his attraction to the novel without a central character or with a collective protagonist. All this, however, requires qualification in the light of *Los pasos perdidos*. Here the narrator is an ambiguous, self-aware human being, with all the qualities and imperfections we expect of a fully rounded fictional character. This is not to say that he is not also symbolic. The son of a Swiss-German Protestant father and a Cuban Catholic mother, he represents the two major Western religious and racial groups. Born in Latin America, an emigrant to the United States with two long stays in Europe, he is doubly the product of both Latin American and Anglo-Saxon cultures. In addition he is an artist, a composer, "a maniacal measurer of time, heeding the metronome by vocation and the chronograph as part of my job."[3] At this level he symbolizes both Western man and the artist in Western society. To the extent that the artist is traditionally seen as a specially significant representative of his people or of his generation, the role of the narrator as artist intensifies his role as a kind of archetype. At this more abstract level what characterizes the narrator is his alienation. As in all Carpentier's major works, the first chapter of this twice-rewritten novel has many meanings, starting from the initial phrase, which is a time-notation. Although at first the opening seems to deal with the situation of the narrator's actress wife, Ruth, it is in fact designed to prefigure his own awareness of being trapped in a robotlike life of falsehood and repetition. As a man, he is "caught in a surrounding from which there was no escape, exasperated by not being able to change anything in my existence, governed always by the will of others, who scarcely left me the freedom, each morning, to choose the meat or cereal I prefer for breakfast" (20). As an artist, having given up his true creative vocation out of disgust, poverty, and readiness to put his wife's career first, he is reduced to writing music for commercials. The result is a feeling of futility, automatism, solitude, and total subjection to time. This brings classic neurotic symptoms: anxiety, insomnia, lack of satisfaction in sexuality, indecision, and longing to escape.

In all this he is aware that his is part of a general malaise, that of "the era of the Wasp-Man, the Human Nobody, in which souls are not sold to the Devil, but to the Accountant or the Overseer" (14). New York, and implicitly all Western urban society, is seen as enslaved to purely commercial values in which the human personality is ignored or exploited in peace and exterminated in war.

Its heritage of art is debased; its culture is seen as charlatanism pervaded by anguish. Sex and alcohol provide pseudofulfillment. The picture reflects the perennial Latin American will to believe that European and North American civilization is in an irremediable decline, an impulse stimulated afresh by the spectacle of Europe in the 1930s and by isolationist America. The horrors of the Second World War, reflected in the mention of the narrator's visit to a Nazi extermination camp, seemed to provide confirmation of the bankruptcy of the West, already forecast by Spengler and accepted by Carpentier in his "Dusk of Europe" articles in the 1940s. The central ironic symbol of Western moral and cultural decay in the novel is Beethoven's Ninth Symphony, with its exaltation of joy and the brotherhood of man. For the narrator it is associated with the death camp: "I could never have imagined," he comments, "so absolute a bankruptcy of Western Man" (96). Only Latin America offers new hope.

But the narrator of *Los pasos perdidos* stands out by virtue of the way his archetypal or representative function meshes with his self-presentation as a convincing human being at the emotional and psychological level. Typical here, for example, is subchapter 11, in which he steps completely out of his symbolic role and emerges as a diffident and rather insecure male in a society where courtship follows a quite different pattern from the one he knows. He is tempted to make a pass at his new acquaintance, Rosario, but cannot bring himself to the point of doing so. His fear of ridicule and his uneasy preoccupation with what the girl might be thinking of his obligations to his mistress, Mouche (feelings that are partly an alibi for his inaction and partly a guilt-reaction), strike an immediate chord of sympathy in every male reader and bring the narrator totally alive. Alive, that is, as a typical antihero of modern fiction. What makes such figures attractive and original is their contrast to the nineteenth-century fictional hero. The narrator here has that touch of ignobility that makes us all kin; that repressed, betrayed, better nature; that insecurity, that sneaking self-contempt, just too easily placated; that minimum of aspiration hidden behind layers of not-too-successful self-deception, in which we recognize ourselves. What above all is part of his bedrock character, and what survives his experiences in the jungle, is his weakness, his characteristic and all-too-human inability not just to make sacrifices, but to make enough sacrifices.

But here, as art takes over from Carpentier's ideology, and the narrator's character ceases to be schematic and symbolic of Western man and the modern artist, a problem appears. For to the extent that the narrator has such individual, nonrepresentative qualities as those of weakness, guilt-feeling, and desire for self-justification, his reliability as a commentator on himself and his experiences becomes suspect. How do we know that the influences he describes as responsible for this rootlessness, his alienation—the oppression of society, his wartime experiences, the debased culture he has absorbed—are not part of an elaborate mechanism of self-excuse? If they are, this helps to explain the naive oversimplifications, the black and white contrasts, that seem to flaw the novel. Perhaps, at the level of the narrator as an individual, we are reading an account of a prolonged delusion. Macdonald, in what is by far the most perceptive article on the narrator, emphasizes "the intricate and treacherous structure" of the background against which the latter's comments on the cultural influences operating on him are set. "We are faced," Macdonald suggests, "with an orthodox unreliable narrator, with the ironic subversion of his account."[4]

At the heart of the novel lies one of Carpentier's most characteristic ironies. The narrator's journey into the jungle, originally undertaken in bad faith, rapidly turns into a pilgrimage, the shrine being authenticity, the achievement of a new, liberated, and serene personality. But paradoxically, reaching the ideal in Santa Mónica is found to involve the adoption of a social function. "They all, with their hands, with their vocations, fulfill a destiny. The hunter hunts, the friar teaches religion, the *Adelantado* governs. Now it is I who must also have a job" (231). As a composer, the narrator's vocation is to compose; but such activity is irrelevant to this community, and anyway an adequate supply of pens and paper is lacking. Thus what constitutes the very kernel of authenticity, truth to one's vocation, proves to be impossible in the very shrine of authenticity itself—but only if one is a creative artist. Even as a mere performer, an entertainer, the narrator could have had a role in Santa Mónica. It is creativity that is impossible. At this point the two representative functions of the narrator diverge. As a contemporary man he could, theoretically at least, find refuge from the pressures of the modern world in a more "natural" life in a primitive society. But as an artist, such refuge is denied him. For as Müller-Bergh affirms, "according to Carpentier the destiny of the intellectual consists in the struggle itself, in being a witness and a prophet for the men of his time."⁵

The beginning and end of the novel, set in New York, create a picture of modern urban life that not only turns the city's inhabitants into miserable automata but also (and this is why chapter 1 begins with actors trapped in an endlessly repeated play) makes them inauthentic and artificial. Expressive of this artificiality are the narrator's wife, Ruth, whom we later discover is incapable of anything but role-playing even in real life, and his mistress, Mouche, who earns her living by astrology. Both women provide commercialized illusion. Mouche is the more important, which is unfortunate, for she is one of Carpentier's least successful characters, being deplorably unsubtle. Every single reference to her is derogatory in one sense or another. She is a fake who lives by deception and fools even herself. Her culture is a grotesque parody of the narrator's (which allows Carpentier to set up an ironic relationship between them at this level), her sexual life is promiscuous and her spontaneous outlook is dishonest. As the basis of the narrator's character is weakness, so hers is a "demanding and selfish animality" (29), which leads from suspected lesbianism with the Canadian painter in subchapter 7 to her provocation of Yannes in subchapter 10 and finally to her lesbian overture to Rosario in subchapter 17.

As a character in her own right Mouche is completely sacrificed to her triple function in the narrative. First she is there to provide emphasis by means of contrast. Her downward evolution from mere charlatanism in New York to moral and physical collapse in the jungle is employed to point up the opposite evolution of the narrator, with whom she shares the privilege of being one of the only two characters who actually evolve at all. Her second function, when she reappears at the end, is to destroy the imposture built around the narrator by his wife and to prevent the sale of his falsified account of his trip. Thus she largely creates the circumstances that undermine his newfound sense of authenticity and prevent his return to Santa Mónica until it is too late. Mouche's third function, reinforced by Ruth, is to contrast with Rosario. While her superficial cosmopolitanism, phonyness, and immorality express the degeneracy of the "old" European and North American civilization, Rosario, "a living summation of races" (84), since she is partly white, partly Indian, and partly Negro, represents the "new" Latin American component of the human family, the "cosmic race" dreamed of by the Mexican Vasconcelos.

The first two features of Rosario's character are carefully selected to underline the two extremes of her personality: her simple acceptance of danger and discomfort in the hope of relieving her father's sufferings (typical of the stoic fortitude of "authentic" people), and her closeness to nature, visible in her knowledge of herbs and in her respect for the forces of nature. Both are in strict contrast to Mouche's intolerance of discomfort and her complex, commercialized superstitions. Rosario's character is built up subsequently by dint of further contrasts with Mouche. While the latter reads modern, literary pornography, Rosario reads a simple, traditional folktale, which she accepts as both true and contemporary. She has no concept of the past and hence of time. She represents the true escape from time: life in the continuous present. It has also been suggested that her name, Rosario, connects her with Santa Rosa of Lima and that she represents Latin America in a spiritual sense, converting the narrator's quest into something semireligious rather than merely existential. But this is doubtful, though the narrator's wish to buy a rosary shortly after reaching Latin America may be relevant.

By the middle of subchapter 10 the contrast between Rosario and Mouche is virtually complete. Mouche is eccentric and out of place in the jungle; Rosario is ever more authentic, adjusted to her surroundings and invested with an aura of "innate dignity." A bond of sympathy soon exists between her and the narrator, signaling and hastening his evolution. In the course of subchapter 14, by her father's coffin, she attains an almost tragic grandeur, which for Carpentier is evidently related to something fundamental in man's response to death. Finally her simple carnality contrasts with Mouche's perversion. Rosario is the "woman of the Earth" (178), "a complete woman, without being more than a woman" (197). Like Mouche, with whom the contrast is too systematic and extreme, she remains unconvincing. Rosario is a man's ideal of a woman when he is in certain moods: the woman who creates no complications, who is not clever enough to see through him, who is carnal enough to satisfy him, but who has none of those irritating feminine characteristics of possessiveness, emotional extortion, insecurity, vanity, jealousy, and obliqueness, which offset the rest. What Rosario lacks to make her real is that imperious demand for emotional support, which is such a prominent feminine characteristic. The fact is that both Mouche and Rosario exist primarily in relation to the narrator, rather than as autonomous characters.

The contrast between them is reflected in the two groups of minor characters flanking them. Around Mouche are the other representatives of the decadent urban intelligentsia: Extieich, the forger of works of art; the Canadian lesbian; and the three Latin American artists who are criticized for their obsession with Europe and their blindness to their own "marvelous real." Around Rosario are set the Adelantado and his son, Fray Pedro, Yannes, and the people of the jungle generally, whose mentality is described in terms of detachment from materialism, fidelity to "a more honest and valid culture, probably, than the one that remained back there" (123), courage, stoicism, and closeness to nature. The critical question about the ideological thrust of the novel and its expression in contrasting groups of characters is whether it is intended to be taken at face value, or whether it is meant to be read as indicative of the way the narrator (as distinct from the author) sees things. There has been too little discussion of this vital point, but it has to be made. The picture of New York is a caricature. The narrator's situation is no more typical of that of the modern artist than Mouche and her circle are representative of modern culture. The presentation of the Adelantado, his group, and the way of life in Santa Mónica is patently idealized. Individual virtue and happiness are largely independent of time and place. The quality of life in a great conurbation is not necessarily worse than in the jungle; the problems are simply of a different order. As it is, reality in *Los pasos perdidos* seems to have been trimmed to fit a simplified pattern. To take only the most obvious example, how much more interesting the narrator's position would have been if he had been presented with a real choice—if, that is, Mouche had represented the complementary values to those of Rosario, such as intellectual companionship and genuine comprehension. But that would have involved admitting that modern urban society had something to offer.

This brings us back to the narrator and the problem of the ending. The first stage in the latter's self-introduction stresses his devitalized existence in New York, followed by his acceptance of Mouche's plan to swindle the university. But paradoxically it is this very act of weakness that leads him to begin to recover the ability to live properly once more, portended by the epigraph to chapter 2: "Ha! I scent life." The fifteen streetlamps of Los Altos lead from a bar and a brothel to three crosses on the brow of a nearby hill, and are specifically declared to have an allegorical meaning. They point the way to faith, which Carpentier repeatedly stresses is an important ingredient of authentic existence. But, despite the views of some critics, it is faith in life's possibilities rather than religious faith as such. At length in the jungle the narrator recovers this sort of faith. Part of the process is his success in overcoming the double test of fear in subchapters 19 and 21, after which he is rewarded with the peak of his idyll with Rosario. But he is never fully at ease in Santa Mónica. He is a misfit there, unable either to emancipate himself from intellectual preoccupations or to suppress his creativity. Long before he fails the third test (the punishment of the leper rapist) his sense of being able to live in the settlement is close to self-deceit. As an artist, he recognizes on the last page of the novel, he cannot turn his back on his own times. As a representative of humanity also, he must look ahead, not backwards to primitivism. Carpentier has stated that "the end of my novel, the moral, so to speak, affirms that man, in order to be man and fulfill himself, can never escape from his own epoch, even though he may be offered the means of such escape."[6]

How then are we to interpret the ending? *Los pasos perdidos* chronicles a journey of self-discovery; but what, in the end, does the narrator discover? Carpentier tells us that the river in the novel symbolizes historical time; as one ascends it, one passes from the present into the past. In fact the narrator passes from the nineteenth century in provincial Latin America to the Conquest period during the first river journey, and, eventually, through the Stone Age of the jungle Indians, to the world of prehistory. Here once more we are in the domain of the marvelous real of Latin America, where different historical periods appear to exist side by side. At the level of inner awareness, the narrator discovers that men can escape from the modern world and find greater authenticity, but only briefly. Santa Mónica itself is not outside time. It already has laws, punishments, obligations, a Church, a ruling class. It is not a true refuge. But, like Ti Noel, the narrator, though granted insight through his various experiences, is not allowed to act on it. The novel ends ambiguously with his reflection: "It remains to be seen whether I shall be deafened and deprived of my voice by the hammer-strokes of the Overseer who somewhere awaits me" (273).

Two interpretations are possible. Either the failure of the narrator to act on the awareness he has acquired that "the greatest work proposed to the human being is that of forging for himself a destiny" (251), i.e., accepting his "Task," suggests the futility of struggling against the human condition; or, less pessimistically, it implies, like the failure of revolutionary endeavor in *El reino de este mundo* and *El siglo de las luces,* that human weakness is always present as a factor retarding progress, but not preventing it entirely. Similarly, with regard to the narrator himself, his inability to cleave to a "true" self, and the muddle and contradictions of his outlook, so well analyzed by Macdonald, seem to reveal a character "in bad faith." Nor can we disagree with González Echevarría's postulate of an ironic intention in Carpentier that progressively distances us as readers from the narrator.[7] But what does this mean? Again we can take it both ways. It can mean that modern man deceives himself with a dream of authenticity in the past, but in pursuing it, merely moves from alienation to self-delusion and back again. Or it can mean that the direction was wrong, and that true escape can only be found in the future. The latter option seems more in line with Carpentier's overall standpoint. Critics, however, are completely divided on the issues raised by the ending of *Los pasos perdidos.* Volek, Eduardo González, and Poujol, among others, take a positive view; González Echevarría, Palermo, and others take a negative one; M. I. Adams hovers in between.[8]

The form of *Los pasos perdidos* is that of a first-person memoir covering a few months of what seems to be 1950, with flashbacks to the narrator's childhood and earlier manhood. In brief: an extended monologue. The shape of the narrative is imposed by the narrator's own inner evolution, which in turn is governed by his journey through both space and time. Like Carpentier in his long trip to Europe, the narrator needs to travel in order to discover something about himself. The trip turns into a search for a private Shangri-La, a search that expresses modern man's yearning to escape from the human condition, which the author and the narrator see as increasingly intolerable. Everything is geared to this theme, so that what we have is a carefully arranged series of events, the very selection of which is in itself a form of indirect commentary on the theme, and a group of equally deliberately selected characters deployed functionally around the narrator. At the same time the first-person form allows a continuous interpretation of, and commentary on, the events and characters as they appear, as well as frequent reflections by the narrator on his own evolving outlook. Thus the predominant technical feature is the all-pervading commentary, both direct and indirect, which (in the opinion of Rodríguez Almodóvar, for instance[9]) weighs down the narrative with ideological elements. There is no easy line of demarcation between the narrator as protagonist and the narrator as observer. His commentary is fused with the narrative itself both through his reported thoughts and direct value-judgments and through conversations stage-managed by Carpentier to include commentary. We have already mentioned the use of representative characters: Ruth and Mouche in contrast to Rosario; Fray Pedro and the Adelantado in contrast to Extieich and his companions. But Yannes, the Greek prospector, merits a special place because of the way his own odyssey parallels that of the narrator. Finally the incidents are in many cases designed specifically to underline aspects of the theme. A case in point is offered by those of the narrator's return to New York (the commercialization even of the moral and emotional aspects of his situation, the drunkenness of a colleague at the airport, the farce of the reception party), which are intended to stress the contrast with life in Santa Mónica. The reader may care to try this test: to think of an incident in the novel that resists ideological interpretation. The result is that we come dangerously close to asking ourselves not "What happens next?" but "What will be the meaning of what happens next?"

Finally we must not overlook the role played in the novel by the mythical references and foreshadowing devices. Carpentier makes use of three, possibly four, well-known myths: those of Sisyphus, of Prometheus, and of Ulysses, and the last, associated both with the narrator and with Yannes, links their journeys to an archetypal journey, which includes, in the narrator's case, a reluctant departure from a place of bliss and an ironic homecoming. It confers a special stature on the journey motif. The myths of Sisyphus and Prometheus, on the other hand, relate to the narrator's break with his life in New York: i.e., to Sisyphus's being able to cease his labors or to Prometheus's being unchained from his rock. King[10] makes a very plausible case for a hidden Orpheus myth underlying all. In terms of it, the narrator-as-Orpheus includes in his quest the search for liberation from death and hell via art. The key reference is to the shaman in subchapter 23 as an Orphic magician. The function of the myths, rather than contributing to the "organization" of the novel, as Müller-Bergh rather obscurely suggests,[11] is to dignify the narrator and his story by lending them timeless associations. The main foreshadowing device is the description of the narrator's visit to a gallery of reproductions of famous art treasures at the end of subchapter 3. This produces an excursus through romantic and renaissance art to medieval, Dark Age, preclassical, and ultimately prehistoric art, before Goya's picture of Chronos (Time) devouring his children brings the narrator back to the present. This unwinding of time is precisely what the narrator is about to experience at first hand. Again, the early reference to Santa Rosa of Lima seems to point forward to the meeting with Rosario, just as the desire of the narrator to buy a copy of the *Odyssey* portends the gift of the book by Yannes.

The basic plot structure: that of a frustrated quest, which begins and ends in the same place, has by its very nature three phases. There is the ignominy of chapter 1; the achievement of psychic and spiritual balance in the jungle, ironically offset by a revival of the urge to create; and the return to ignominy, perhaps with greater insight, at the end. The first ten of the thirty-nine subchapters occupy some two-fifths of the entire text. Thereafter only one sub-chapter stands out by reason of length: that of the narrator's return to New York. But the average length of the subchapters tends to increase toward the end of the novel. Thus we have a certain concentration of material at each end, with a slight change of rhythm in the middle. The focal points at each end are the narrator's agreement to swindle the university in subchapter 3 and his seduction by Mouche after his return. The center of the novel comprises subchapters 11 through 32 (twenty-two subchapters, but only as much actual text as the first ten) with its own center of balance in subchapter 22. Here the first stage of the external plot ends, with the acquisition of the instruments. In the next chapter the second stage begins with the discovery of Santa Mónica. This stage in turn concludes with the beginning of subchapter 33: the arrival of the plane to take the narrator back to New York. The last six subchapters bring his odyssey full circle, but leave us guessing whether he will retain anything of what he has learned in the jungle.

To conclude: the theme of *Los pasos perdidos* is connected with the contrast between two modes of existence; one is characterized by anguish, monotony, and frustration, the other by serenity and self-fulfillment. In other words the novel is about the authentic and the

inauthentic life. The link between them is time. The inauthentic
life is dominated by the struggle against time, the inauthentic people
are trapped and tyrannized by time, the enemy. The authentic
people, by contrast, have little sense of time; they live in a continuous present symbolized by the change to the present-tense diary
form of the narrative in subchapter 16 when the narrator adopts
their life-style. E. González[12] stresses the very careful time-notations
beginning on Sunday, 4 June 1950 and ending on Saturday, 30
December of that year, the middle year of the century. The narrator
can be seen to have lived through a series of symbolic weeks. But
perhaps what matters most is that, shortly before shifting the narrative into the continuous present, the narrator begins to forget the
sequence of days of the week, "a forgetfulness that announces his
liberation," González comments. Time, then, is one of the basic
agglutinants of *Los pasos perdidos.* In contrast to Carpentier's cyclic
or spiral view of time, here there seems to be a longing for a timeless
dimension in which to live secure from historical change. But it is
an unattainable aspiration.

Chapter Five
Three Stories of Sanctuary

El acoso

The end of *Los pasos perdidos* carried the date 6 January 1953 and the novel was published in the same year. *El acoso,* though dated 20 February 1955, was apparently ready for printing by December 1954, but did not appear until 1956. Carpentier once boasted that, after a long gestation, the actual writing had only taken ten days. Be that as it may, this is one of his most complex works. It is the story of the last days of a young terrorist involved in armed attacks on representatives of the Machado regime in Cuba in the early 1930s. Arrested after a bombing incident, his confession has led to the deaths of several comrades. Having been released and taken refuge with his old nurse, he is forced back on to the streets by her sudden death. Seeking sanctuary first with a prostitute, Estrella, and later in a church, he fails to obtain official protection and is recognized by two men. They follow him to a concert hall and shoot him at the end of a performance of Beethoven's *Eroica* Symphony.

The germ of the idea, according to the author, was a similar shooting he witnessed during a performance of Aeschylus's *The Choephori* in the courtyard of the University of Havana. But the resulting novella is far more than an evocation of the violence of the period. Its theme is betrayal and expiation. At the surface level, the central incident is the betrayal in prison of his fellow urban guerrillas by the unnamed protagonist. But this betrayal, partly justified by threats of atrocious tortures, is inseparable from other, more significant acts of treachery. On his arrival in Havana as a student, the youth had gravitated toward orthodox Marxism, accepting a Communist party card and joining a party cell. But the behavior of the regime had thrust him toward direct action and the "terrible game" of political assassination. In retrospect he realizes that his party card was "the last barrier that could have kept him from the abomination";[1] but "from this too he had become a renegade" (227). Once involved in direct action, he had become aware of his treachery

to the ideals of the guerrillas themselves: "the first fury, the oath
to avenge the fallen comrades, the HOC ERAT IN VOTIS coming to
mind in front of the corpses of the condemned, turned into a job
with quick earnings and protectors in high places" (243). Behind
the betrayal of his comrades lies the betrayal not only of the "true"
revolutionary group, the Communist party, but also of the very
ideals for which he had been ready to kill. Behind these again lies
the betrayal of himself, of his own ability to think and understand,
instead of blindly accepting the clap-trap that had served for a time
to justify his actions. All these are compounded in a final act of
betrayal, this time of love and compassion, when, given shelter by
his nurse at great risk to herself, he steals her last bit of food as she
lies dying.

Already we can see that Carpentier is concerned with much more
than treachery to a political cause. For the theme is expanded to
embrace one after another of the supporting characters. "All the
other characters betray or deceive, some intentionally, some un-
wittingly," Frances Weber writes. "Estrella, the Becario, the taxi-
driver, the police inspector."[2] She might have added also the priest
and even the nurse's niece, who hurries away from the dying woman
to see her boyfriend. Without doubt the two figures who most
clearly reemphasize the theme are the ticket-office clerk at the concert hall, "whose function in the novel is to echo, as if in a minor
key, the theme of fall from original innocence,"[3] and Estrella, the
prostitute.

The story opens not with the terrorist, but with the ticket-seller
behind his metal grille, reading the life of Beethoven before the
performance begins, but finding his attention fixed on a rich woman
concertgoer who is cooling her skin against the bars in front of him.
The exposition thus centers on the conflict between noble devotion
to music (the clerk is a would-be concert pianist) and lust, which
triumphs when the terrorist, seeking sanctuary in the hall, throws
the clerk a large-denomination banknote. The clerk leaves to spend
the money on Estrella. He is frustrated by the fact that she is out
of sorts because of a visit from the police in search of a suspect and
because she believes the banknote to be a forgery. He returns to the
concert hall ashamed, and longs to visit instead the terrorist's old
nurse, whom he knows by sight and regards as a symbol of the
purity of soul that he has lost. The clerk thereafter disappears until
the last scene, when, with savage irony, Carpentier has him hand

the bill to the policeman, who pockets it knowing it to be legitimate. The terrorist's story is thus deliberately framed by that of the clerk and Estrella.

Since the police apparently question Estrella before she briefly harbors the terrorist and after he has been arrested once and released, it is not clear what they are looking for or what she could have told them about him. The view of King and others that Estrella sets his pursuers on his trail is hard to sustain. What is clear is that she, like him in prison, is intimidated by mere threats and perhaps gives them a clue of some sort. Her expiation is correspondingly harsher than that of the clerk. He is conscious of an ideal betrayed. She is made aware for the first time of the meaning and implications of the word "whore" in all its abjection. The brilliantly conceived functionality of the roles of the clerk and the prostitute is one of Carpentier's triumphs in the masterly narrative strategy of the novella.

Estrella is chiefly seen from the outside, as she reveals herself to the clerk and the terrorist. Only in her moment of bitterest realization do we enter her consciousness. She has no mental flashbacks. The ticket-clerk is similarly presented from the outside, third-person, viewpoint, but from the first we are given a series of flashbacks to his early life, before he had begun to nourish the fantasy of a musical career based on austere self-sacrifice, against which his physical self rebels. These flashbacks to a state of "lost purity," the first of which is significantly associated with the terrorist's old nurse, establish the technique Carpentier uses much more extensively in his treatment of the terrorist himself. The latter is presented in the exposition entirely from the inside, via internal monologue. Thus Carpentier sets up a kind of gradation at the beginning of the novella, in which the degree of "interiority" varies from one character to another.

The central section (part 2) is one vast flashback, beginning a fortnight before the death of the terrorist, while he is in hiding with his nurse. It contains a series of secondary flashbacks to the protagonist's earlier life designed to explain how he got into his present predicament. At this point we find ourselves facing the central critical problem of *El acoso:* that of interpreting the story and the character of the protagonist in terms of their allegorical meaning. Already in the first internal monologue of the young man as he listens to the *Eroica* in the concert hall we are aware of an unusual element. Dizzy with fear and fatigue, he mentally repeats the words of the Creed and reacts as if, in some strange way, the symphony manifested God's judgment of him. We realize later that, while in hiding previously, he had undergone a sudden religious conversion.

It is this religious frame of reference, together with references to Sophocles' *Electra,* quotations from Rolland's biography of Beethoven, and the anecdote associated with the dedication of the symphony, that signals to us that a merely realistic reading of *El acoso* is quite inadequate. Such readings have been made, notably by A. J. Carlos and M. G. Sánchez,[4] with regard to different aspects of the novella. Their conclusions clarify Carpentier's outlook and his fidelity to events of the time. In a letter of 14 April 1972 to a North American student, he asserted that "my central character, who lacks ideological training, who acts without any precise aim in view"[5] could have been saved by holding to the abstentionist policy of the Cuban Communist party, of which he had been briefly a member, in those days. This tends to confirm that Carpentier, at the surface level of the story, was condemning the sort of blind terrorism in which the protagonist was involved, and that we are not intended to sympathize wholly with the latter. At this level *El acoso* can be read as a political fable containing an implicit warning against precipitate armed action by fringe-groups of the left. The allusions to Orestes in the text support this interpretation, since Sophocles was criticizing a similar outlook in him. But for some critics[6] what is basic here is that the protagonist does not see his actions and his predicament in a political light at all.

He interprets them in religious terms. Among the key words in the text are "purity" and "abominable/abomination." The protagonist regards himself as having fallen away from the state of grace and purity associated with his childhood and his nurse into an abomination of sin. But during his stay with his nurse he is granted a redemptive vision. As the old woman lifts a burning brand from the fire (the reference to Amos 4:11 is patent), he suddenly realizes the need to accept an Ultimate Cause, the origin of fire and of all things. A devotional book strengthens his awareness. This is why he perceives the *Eroica* in terms of a meeting with God as his judge. Critics from Weber and Volek onward have stressed the religious references to the liturgy, quotations from the Creed and mentions of God and the Virgin, the facts that the protagonist was born in Sancti Spiritus, that the main events take place on Easter Sunday, and that the concert hall is indirectly presented as a temple. We also notice the similarity between the terrorist's wandering across the center of Havana and the religious exercise of visiting the Stations of the Cross. In 1975 Carpentier was rather dismissive of this aspect of the novella.[7] But, like the comments he made at this time on Esteban in *El siglo de las luces*, this one perhaps should be taken with caution.

The value of this approach to *El acoso* lies in the way it brings out the allegorical substructure of the work. But it involves difficulties. Mocega-González, for instance, who carries the approach to an extreme, avoids any serious mention of the protagonist's attempt to seek sanctuary and absolution in a church, without success, or the notation that his gesture of crossing himself was "a useful exercise." The whole question of Carpentier's religious outlook is a vexing one. Although on occasion, as in the cases of Rosario and Fray Pedro in *Los pasos perdidos*, he presents orthodox religious belief favorably, elsewhere he deals harshly both with the Church and its teachings. Certainly he seems to credit positive beliefs as a factor in human progress, but these beliefs are not necessarily religious or orthodox. To view him at any stage in his career, as Graciela Maturo does,[8] as "adhering profoundly to a secularized Christianity," is misleading. In the case of *El acoso*, therefore, the religious allegory the novella contains may be intended to be seen ironically. Weber is led into contradiction by failing to take account of this. She was the first to develop the idea that *El acoso* contains an "allegorical scheme of transgression and punishment," but she also sees the characters' roles as interchangeable, which "denied them individual behavior." It is not clear how notions of transgression and punishment, much less sin and atonement, can apply to such robots, except ironically. The facts that the terrorist is converted when in a state of desperation, that he is denied absolution by a priest, and that he associates repentance with escape from his pursuers seem to indicate that we must approach the religious dimension of the novella with great care. A final difficulty arises from the terrorist's sense that all is predestined. For those critics who hold that Carpentier is a skeptical fatalist for whom history holds only repetition, there is no problem. But we have seen that there is evidence to contradict this view. If we accept Carpentier's assertion that man, despite repeated failures, is able by painful effort to improve his condition on earth, the protagonist's sense of fatality, like his turning to God, becomes an alibi to avoid responsibility.

A feature of "new" fiction in Latin America is its tendency to stress the multiplicity of the real and to respond to it, among other ways, by abandoning the linear, immediately comprehensible pattern of the traditional novel, by subverting chronological time order, by avoiding omniscient narration, and by expanding the symbolic and allegorical content of novels. All these features are present in *El acoso,* which has been described as "bewildering" and "labyrinthine."[9] The critical questions are: Does the presentation of reality in this way really relate to the author's vision of a world that is more chaotic (and hence less the product of divine design) than used to be believed, or is it merely a gimmick? Second, does the new kind of narrative organization respond to an artistic intention and produce a more satisfying fictional artefact than a more traditional story arrangement would?

The first question is very difficult to answer in view of Carpentier's later evolution. The apparent jumbling of incidents may reflect a general loss of confidence in our ability to perceive meaningful patterns in reality. Equally there is the emphasis on broken decorations, peeling paint, rubbish, grotesque juxtapositions of columns without architectural unity or purpose, and above all the possible symbolism of the house, which had been the headquarters of the terrorist group, now demolished (the regime systematically blew up terrorist hideouts). These all convey an impression of chaotic disorder, decay, and collapse, which is at one with the disorder of the protagonist's outlook, the decay of his ideals, and the collapse of his personality. But they may also express Carpentier's awareness of the collapse of an older, more confident, and more orderly worldview. With this qualification, however: the time progression of the flashbacks in the main section of the narrative is generally chronological, starting with the terrorist's arrival in Havana and ending with his confession in prison. This at least partially invalidates Weber's notion of Carpentier's "war on time," which is in fact far less radical than, say, the Mexican Juan Rulfo's in *Pedro Páramo.* It may also contain the implication that what is crumbling is the old social order and with it the pre-Marxist view of man's situation. It is questionable whether Carpentier's conscious outlook went much further than this, except sporadically.

The greater effectiveness of the present arrangement of the narrative can easily be seen by comparing it to the chronological account of the same events. By compelling the reader to reconstruct these, Carpentier exploits our active pleasure in puzzle-solving and at the same time involves us in the process of storytelling. If we next examine the opening, for instance, we recognize that the unexpected insertion of the terrorist's first-person monologue between the two ticket-clerk sequences produces a superb dramatic effect, like a sudden change of key. We have already mentioned the ticket-clerk sequences as a framing device to set the scene for the final killing, to introduce Estrella, and to set up a parallelism between the clerk and the terrorist, which is reinforced by their joint response to the old nurse as a symbol of purity. The main technical feature of the thirteen unnumbered sequences of the central section of *El acoso* is the way in which Carpentier contrives to blend together narration and allegory. His other major problem was that of knitting together in a nonmechanical way the two time-strands. On the one hand these sequences begin with the terrorist's hiding out with his nurse and end, after his recognition by his killers, with his flight into the concert hall. On the other hand, intercalated, are a series of flashbacks that carry us from the arrival of the terrorist in Havana as a young student, through his urban guerrilla activities, to his arrest and confession. The allegorical dimension is created, as we have seen, by extending the pattern of betrayal and atonement to other characters, by the religious elements, and by the references to Orestes. At the same time the symphony serves to comment not only on the protagonist's treachery, by implicitly comparing it to Napoleon's betrayal of French revolutionary ideals, but perhaps also on the genuineness of the young man's conversion. His religious feelings and the symphony, both in the second sequence of the opening and in the fourth sequence of the central section, are significantly juxtaposed, the noble music of the symphony may be intended to offset ironically the protagonist's retreat into religious feelings as a form of self-excuse.

The actual knitting together of the time-strands is very skillfully executed. The first two important flashbacks deal with the protagonist's arrival in Havana, his evolution to terrorism, and his arrival at the nurse's house in fear of death: i.e., the beginning and the end of his career as a terrorist. These are followed by the Estrella sequence, in which there are no flashbacks. The most extensive temporal regression occurs in sequences 8 through 11, with a climax in sequence 9, when the narration passes once more suddenly into the first person for the trial by the terrorists of an earlier informer. This marks the transition from heroic terrorism to corrupt terrorism. The tense of the narration also changes, to the present; but the circumstances narrated, leading up to the accusation, are in the past. In contrast, in the tenth sequence, which is once more in the past tense, there is a brief return to present-tense stream of thought, containing memories of the end of the trial of the first informer, once more referring to the past. In other words, at the climax of this part of the novella, the shuffling of interior/exterior narration and present/past time reaches its maximum complexity, riveting our attention on this critical point of shift.

The last two sequences of the central section of *El acoso* avoid anticlimax by means of more irony. In sequence 8 the terrorist notices the nearby Communist party headquarters and hears the threatening words of the choir in *Electra,* portending his death. Between the two he crosses himself. As he leaves prison in section 11 his eye is caught by the churches, and in the next sequence he enters a church to seek absolution but is rebuffed. The references to the party headquarters just before the climax of betrayal and to the church after it is another framing device designed to set the main episode of cowardice between the "true" option (the party line) and the "false" option, in which he tries to find refuge after informing on his comrades. Finally, in the thirteenth sequence, his meeting with the Becario, who insists on congratulating him for what he now most wishes to obliterate from his past, completes a ferociously ironic coda.

The ending of the novella is in two contrasting sequences. In the first we are brought back into the thoughts of the terrorist as he listens to the symphony. A shooting in which he had participated provides him with an imaginary scenario for his own murder, as he interprets the scherzo in terms of a blessing on his pursuers. For the last time Carpentier ironically links past and present and weaves in the musical and religious commentary. Now the protagonist perceives the concert hall as a church in which mass is just ending. This religious image is the prelude to his final illusion, that of escaping by hiding in the empty hall.

The last sequence reintroduces the ticket-clerk to complete the frame before the murder of the terrorist-informer climaxes the narrative as a whole. But the comment on the symphony's finale seems to imply that the young man's death will be swallowed up in the triumph of the ideals he has betrayed. Much as been made of Carpentier's remark that the novella is in sonata form; but attempts to analyze it on this basis have been more ingenious than convincing. Still, *El acoso* remains Carpentier's most formally complex work. While writing it he asserted in a journalistic article that "it is necessary to invent new forms, bringing into effect that supreme creative aspiration briefly expressed by André Malraux in his admirable phrase: 'every work of art is, initially, a struggle between fixed form and form in process of gestation' . . . today, for the novelists and short-story writers of this continent, the difficult, gestatory, hour has struck of beginning to find for themselves new expressions, new forms, new solutions to literary problems."[10] He was leading the way.

"El derecho de asilo" (Right of Sanctuary)

Dating the periods of composition of Carpentier's works after *El siglo de las luces* is far from easy. In an interview in 1973 he stated that he had already begun to assemble materials for *El recurso del método* and *Concierto barroco* as he was finishing *El siglo de las luces.* This González Echevarría interprets as referring to the late 1950s.[11] As we know, he had written a fragment of what was to become a late chapter of *La consagración de la primavera* (The rite of spring) in the early 1960s. So far as "El derecho de asilo" is concerned, González Echevarría in a surprising oversight gives the date of publication wrongly as 1972, but in his bibliography recognizes that the first Spanish edition was in fact that of 1967, something Janney in his bibliography omits. The story, as both critics realize, first appeared in the French-language version of *Guerra del tiempo* (Paris, 1967), bearing the dateline "Havana, 6 May 1965." If this date is reliable, it is interesting, for it seems clear that "El derecho de asilo" prefigures aspects of the final version of *El recurso del método,* the main writing of which is supposed to have taken place between 1971 and 1973. The theme and the (for Carpentier) novel tone of satirical humor are very similar. In a more similar way still, both works use the same phrase borrowed from Miranda about "un siglo de cuartelazos, bochinches, golpes de estado" (a century of military uprisings, commotions, and coups d'état) and refer condescendingly in an identical way to the Latin American tendency to attribute highly miraculous powers to local images of the Virgin. Ricardo, the protagonist of "El derecho de asilo," is plainly closely related to the figure of Peralta in *El recurso del método*. Finally, both works use the same technique of unexpected shifts of the narrative voice from first to second and third person, in addition to sudden shifts of time.

The story is that of the right-hand man of a president of an imaginary republic in the northern part of South America who barely escapes capture during a military takeover and seeks refuge in the embassy of a contiguous state. There he gradually becomes indispensable, adopts the nationality of the state in question, intervenes successfully in a border dispute between the two states, and also manages to seduce the ambassador's wife. Finally he supplants the former ambassador in his post and is accepted, with reasonably good grace, by the corrupt military dictator who had carried out the original coup.

The story, then, is an amusingly satirical, but also at times bitterly sarcastic, attack on some of the more ludicrous aspects of political administration in Latin America. There is no lack of fiction in the subcontinent concerned with the corridors of power, but much of it has been in the form of frontal attacks on oppressive presidentialism and open dictatorship. Writers in this tradition criticized abuses of power in one of the few ways possible in countries where the mass media were normally heavily censored (we notice the dictator's threat in this story to gag the press if it dares to reveal the casualties caused by a mock air raid). Hence the tone of their works was usually fiercely indignant and serious, if not actually solemn. More recently, however, with the gradual advent of humor into major Latin American fiction, attempts have been made to discredit the oligarchs by means of caricature. Carpentier's own *El recurso del método* is a noteworthy example. "El derecho de asilo" also belongs to this trend. An undertone of deep seriousness of course survives.

One of Carpentier's problems in writing the story was to prevent the caricature from becoming too lighthearted and thus allowing his imaginary (but in fact all too realistic) Latin American state to turn into a comic-operetta Ruritania. It approaches this level at intervals. In an opening vignette we meet Sergeant Ratón of the presidential palace guard, who spends his pay on lettuce for his pet tortoise and candy for the local children. Later we encounter the ambassador, who opens the embassy door himself in his pajamas to admit the fugitive. Finally, when Ricardo reappears at the palace with his letters of accreditation, he is wearing the ex-ambassador's tall hat stuffed with paper. But these elements of low comedy, while they poke gentle fun at the stock figure of the presidential "gorilla" or at the legendary unprofessionality of some Latin American diplomats, also contrast functionally with the seriousness of the situation, in which protesters against the army coup are shot down or tortured, and shrapnel from antiaircraft guns is allowed to rain down on slum shacks with cardboard roofs, killing and maiming even children. The implication is obvious: it is partly because of the frivolity, incapacity, and cynicism of the state apparatus that things go on the way they do. Similarly the alert reader notices that while the state and its neighbor prepare the silly hostilities over the border dispute, which give Ricardo his chance to intervene, the United States quietly advances its economic domination of the disputed zone itself. The technique of juxtaposition of the parodic and the serious, pointing up the causal relationships among folly, greed, and incompetence among Latin American officials, especially at the top, and their harsh consequences for the man in the street, is consistent throughout the text.

But Carpentier does not wholly avoid the classical ambiguity that attends protest of this sort, whether satirical or serious. The weight of the attack falls on members of the state apparatus. But in chapter 4, à propos of the border dispute, Carpentier introduces a parodic thumbnail history of Latin America. This is seen in terms of a greedy rabble of ragged Spanish conquistadors, lawyers, and settlers in the colonial period, followed by a century and a half of bloody rebellions and dictatorships thereafter. The masses are fanaticized by alternate appeals to maximalist libertarian ideals and to golden-haired, sexually attractive, miracle-working images of the Virgin, who can be relied on to turn a blind eye to the peccadilloes of her devotees. It is hard not to see in this excursus a certain contempt for the venality, unsophistication, and general inefficiency of the very people whom Carpentier is attempting to defend by satirizing these same characteristics in their military and administrative classes. The reader is left uneasily wondering how effective such protest can ever be, if it involves the implicit recognition that the evil is in some way related to defects in the national character. Dellepiane[12] persuasively interprets the penultimate epigraph of *El recurso del método,* which states that a creeper will never rise higher than the trees that support it, precisely in this sense. Carpentier would presumably have replied that the emergence of new Socialist Man in Latin America would resolve the problem; but there is little to indicate that this process is operating.

A cognate ambiguity is visible in Ricardo himself. Here Carpentier faced the difficulty of making his protagonist sufficiently cynical and opportunistic to be representative of his class of functionaries, while at the same time rendering him attractive enough to hold the reader's sympathy on the one hand and to be acceptable as a commentator on the other. Ricardo, therefore, combines culture, humor, intelligence, taste, and general capacity with less creditable characteristics that prevent his offering a dignified contrast to the rest of the characters. Initially we find him conniving at the recruitment of high-grade prostitutes for the president's bed and dreaming of wearing the president's insignia himself. Later we find him in bed with the ambassador's wife and seriously considering how to render her speedily a widow. Ultimately in a diplomatic coup, which intentionally reflects the Byzantine maneuvers of Latin American politics, just as the military coup reflects their more brutal side, he ousts his erstwhile predecessor and assumes his post. We notice that it is this discreditable side of his personality that governs his actions in the story and in fact keeps the whole plot moving.

But there is another side to Ricardo. His love of Paul Klee's paintings contrasts with the comic tastelessness of the decorations and furnishings of the presidential palace. His resourcefulness and presence of mind contrast with the brutality and greedy stupidity of the general who seizes power. In particular, beneath his opportunism, there survives a libertarian conscience and aspiration that make him feel guilty as he watches a student demonstration being brutally crushed by the police and recalls his own youthful left-wing affiliations. These more attractive characteristics allow Ricardo to fulfill his role as an inside observer and commentator set in a strategic position just below the top echelon of the political power structure.

A third element of ambiguity is provided by the shifting tenses of the story. Events inside the embassy tend to be told in the present and imperfect tenses, while the preterit is mainly reserved for events that take place outside. Both Delprat and Mason[13] emphasize the elements of intemporality in the work, the latter analyzing cogently the way in which the use of the present tense especially reinforces the other factors (the unchanging litany, the electric train running always around the same circle of track, the Donald Duck toy, the references to the days of the week) that emphasize the unchanging and timeless nature of Ricardo's situation. He is in the same limbo ("tiempo detenido") in which Sofía in *El siglo de las luces* finds herself, between her disillusionment with Hugues and the 1808 rebellion in Madrid, when action once more becomes possible.

A similar reference to time coming to a halt is made in relation to the Dictator in *El recurso del método,* subchapter 8. The question, as always, is how to interpret this recurrent feature of Carpentier's work. In all three works the immobilization of time occurs in regard to significant action. When a bullet knocks Donald Duck off his stand it is a holiday and the shop-assistant is not there to replace the doll. Soon after, Ricardo is able to assume his new nationality and ambassadorial functions, escaping from enforced inaction back into real life. Sofía, too, by leaving for Spain, returns to the world of action again. The Dictator, however, remains trapped. For, though he acts, his actions merely mimic other dictators' actions. Hence he remains outside time, an anachronism. It is possible that Ricardo at the end of "El derecho de asilo" has only exchanged one form of timeless futility, as a refugee, for another, as ambassador of a republic as corrupt as the one he was born in. But timelessness and circularity in Carpentier are not necessarily perceived as inescapable characteristics of the human condition. They are rather seen as related to situations in which progress is betrayed—by Hugues, by the Dictator of *El recurso del método,* or, as here, by Ricardo, who is a progressive at heart. Betrayal of the future, Carpentier implies, is what keeps individuals or societies in a state of timelessness. But, he suggests, revolutionary effort can break out of it, albeit with great difficulty. Sofía, the student in *El recurso del método,* and the couple Enrique/Vera in *La consagración de la primavera* are there to underline this belief on the author's part. It is for the reader to decide whether the whole dichotomy is not a naive simplification of the historical process.

The shift from third-person narration to first and even second person, in and after chapter 2, is designed to let Carpentier alter the focus from outside to inside Ricardo's mind and from middle distance to close-up. Foreshadowed by the narrative technique of *El acoso* and developed on a larger scale in *El recurso del método,* it is highly functional. Mason notes that "the 'second person' narrator is found only in the *Lunes* (Monday) sections and significantly the switch from first to second person narration tends to occur at moments of emotional crisis for the Secretary. It is as if the *yo* (I) cannot face up to these events."[14] Third-person narration is associated closely, but not exclusively, with events outside the embassy, which Ricardo cannot see. In a way that is reminiscent of Foster's interpretation of "El camino de Santiago," Mason argues that one result of the shifting of narrative voices, along with the withholding of Ricardo's name until near the end, is to suggest that he is a kind of Everyman. The commentary is also advantaged. Since part of the story is told using internal monologue, much of the rest of the presentation is more closely associated with Ricardo than it otherwise would be, even when the narrative voice is changed to third person. Thus when it is sarcastically pointed out that the national insignia of the state in whose embassy Ricardo takes refuge shows a white and a black female hand clasping one another, whereas in the country in question white women would not even speak to black women, we actually tend to associate the observation with Ricardo rather than with the narrator. The third-person commentary, that is, tends to retain part of the impact of the first-person reaction we are offered, for instance, when Ricardo at the end of chapter 2 records the corruption and violence that motivate and accompany the change of regime.

As usual in Carpentier, symbolic commentary is prominent. The central symbol is that of a Donald Duck doll in the window of a North American–owned toyshop. At one level the toy stands for the familiar Carpenterian idea of change without progress, which we meet again in "Los advertidos." Each time it is sold the toy is taken from the window and then replaced. It is always different, yet always the same; it stays in one place, yet moves all over the city as the children take it home. It is compared to God: always the same omnipotent figure, yet changing from epoch to epoch. Movement and progress in any sense, of time, of place, of spiritual awareness, are implicitly denied. But concretely the toy comes from a North American shop standing beside a Latin American hardware store. The latter's goods are antiquated and traditional. The former's represent American domination, culturally because Donald Duck has elbowed aside the old familiar Pérez the Mouse of the Hispanic world of childhood; politically because the constant replacement of one Donald Duck by another on its stand represents the replacement of one corrupt regime by another, with North American connivance.

To the Cuban reader "El derecho de asilo" evokes the old order of things, which the Cuban revolution is supposed to have swept away. To the non-Cuban reader, familiar with Latin America, it brings a wry smile of recognition. But the way in which the satiricosymbolic attack on the high officials and their North American support-group involves an implicit critique of the national character (whose best and less attractive features are combined in Ricardo) leaves a note of ambiguity behind. It survives in *El recurso del método*.

"Los advertidos"

Like "El derecho de asilo," "Los advertidos" was first published in 1967 in the French edition of *Guerra del tiempo*. But it bears the dateline 13 June 1965. If this is trustworthy, the final draft must have been finished just after that of "El derecho de asilo," both stories probably belonging to the same creative moment. In view of its origins, which go back to the author's first trip to the interior of Venezuela in 1947, Müller-Bergh[15] has suggested that the story may have been written up to fifteen years earlier. But this is speculation.

In an article in *Carteles*, 22 February 1948, one of the series describing his trip, Carpentier referred to "the universal unity of myths," in which Latin American myths were included. The thought clearly stayed with him, for in *Los pasos perdidos*, chapter 28, he refers again to "the portentous unity of myths." A little earlier he gives a précis of the story that is very similar to the one he had given in the next *Carteles* article (28 March 1948).

Both accounts include the re-creation of man by stones that the Latin American Noah throws behind him. But the account contained in the novel is a step closer to "Los advertidos" because the Noah-figure in it has an ark instead of a dugout canoe as in the *Carteles* version. In neither case, however, is the figure called Amaliwak, though he is referred to in the February *Carteles* article as Amalivaca. "Los advertidos" differs from both earlier sketches by the fact that it is Amaliwak's wife who re-creates mankind by throwing palm-seeds behind her, but much more importantly by the addition of an ironic sequel to the act in which the newly created humanity at once sinks into bloody warfare.

This ending designedly contrasts with the unexpected and astonishing peace and harmony among normally warring tribes, which is emphasized at the beginning. The story tells of how they had been called together by Amaliwak and bribed to build an ark in which he and his family and the usual complement of animals sail away until they meet the Chinese Noah, the Old Testament Noah, Ducalion, and the Egyptian Noah. When each goes his separate way to refound mankind, Amaliwak realizes sadly that "the gods were many. And where there are as many gods as there are peoples, concord can never reign, but rather we must live among disagreements and disorder surrounding everything in the whole universe."[16] When his realization is confirmed by the warfare that immediately breaks out once mankind has been re-created, he concludes that his whole effort in building the ark and repeopling the world has been a waste of time. We recall Esteban's conclusion in *El siglo de las luces*, subchapter 23, that "we are the vilest beasts in creation" and his vision in the next chapter of the "Man of the Totems" instinctively attacking the "Man of Theology."

Clearly, despite Carpentier's conscious belief in, or hope of, a slow, dogged advance of mankind toward a better world, there is a deep pessimism here on two counts. One concerns the nature of man himself, which, from his earliest writings, Carpentier had portrayed as in large measure dominated by lust, cruelty, violence, and fanaticism. The other relates more to the way life is: unregulated by any divine Providence and hence to be thought of in terms of sporadically prevailing decay, disorder, and chaos, which mankind, good or evil, is unable to resist for long. Not surprisingly Müller-Bergh presents the story as totally pessimistic, a parable in which time goes around in endlessly futile circles, the mass of mankind is incapable of improvement, and only a chosen few (the French title of the story is "Les Elus"—"The Elect") can briefly rise above the degradation of the rest. Certainly, if "Los advertidos" is read in isolation from the rest of Carpentier's work, the conclusion cannot be faulted. The various simultaneously existing gods to which the story refers (and we should not overlook the fact that Amaliwak himself accepts two divinities: one kindly and the other whose voice freezes the blood) correspond to the succession of gods who replace one another in Ricardo's musings on the Donald Duck toy in "El derecho de asilo." In both cases what is negated is a single beneficent God. Without such a single providential figure it is understandable that life should seem to be the "nightmare" that Esteban considers it to be as he returns from Cayenne to Havana in *El siglo de las luces*.

But what are we to make of Carpentier's earlier perception that man has an almost metaphysical urge to seek a better life and of the fact that a symbol of life is a spiral shell? Clearly Fornet[17] is correct in his postulate of a negative pole and a positive pole coexisting in fecund contradiction within Carpentier's outlook on life.

Chapter Six
The Antilles Again

El siglo de las luces

In a rarely mentioned article in *Carteles,* 13 March, 1932,[1] Carpentier had expressed impatience with those who go on record about "the inevitable and unstoppable progress of humanity." The article was in reality an attack on the idea of progress as perceived by Hitler and the European Fascist movements, but it is possible to see in it the total rejection of the idea of progress that some critics have seen present in most of Carpentier's work. The publication of *El siglo de las luces* seemed at first sight to mean that fresh evidence was now available that suggested that he saw history statically or as mere cyclical recurrence. But his notion of man imposing tasks on himself remained to complicate the issue. The critical debate about it shows no signs of slackening. A feature of it is the suggestion that Carpentier had modified the text of his new novel, which bore the dateline 1956–58, after his return to Cuba. It has been alleged that he deliberately shifted the emphasis at the end from the disillusioned Esteban to Sofía, who impetuously leads her cousin to join the May 1808 popular uprising in Madrid against the French. More than a decade later he wrote in clarification: "In *El siglo de las luces* the character of Victor Hugues, positive at the start, becomes negative when he embraces the Bonapartist cause. But in the last chapter it is the people of Madrid, who rose against Napoleon on the memorable day recorded by Goya in his most famous picture, who triumph. And in the end it was from Guadeloupe under the governership of Victor Hugues that all the propaganda came that served to light the great burst of flame of the South American Wars of Independence."[2]

How far this may be special pleading is a moot point. But it serves to introduce the theme of *El siglo de las luces.* The story concerns the experiences of Carlos and Sofía, the orphan children of a wealthy Havana merchant, and their cousin Esteban, between 1791 and 1808. Falling under the spell of an adventurer, Victor Hugues,

74

Esteban and Sofía are successively sucked into the mainstream first of the French Revolution and then of its prolongation in the French islands of Guadeloupe and Cayenne. There Hugues reveals himself to be a mere opportunist, mimicking each turn of events in France. Esteban, disillusioned, at last returns to Havana, only to be arrested and deported to Spain for concealing subversive propaganda. Sofía, the real culprit, escapes to join Hugues but is disillusioned in her turn and leaves for Spain, where she and her cousin die fighting the Napoleonic troops in Madrid.

Once more, then, as in *El acoso,* a major theme is the betrayal of the revolutionary ideal. Even the terminology is similar. In *El acoso* we read: "After the times of the Tribunal, came the times of booty," which in *El siglo de las luces* becomes: "The Time of the Trees of Liberty had been followed by the Time of the Scaffolds."[3] But now beside Hugues, who plays on a wider stage the same role as the hunted terrorist, is set Sofía, in whom the libertarian ideal burns brightly to the end, while Esteban incarnates the terrorist's critical hindsight. Similarly, as Labanyi argues,[4] the chaos/order dichotomy, which is very prominent in both works, is here reevaluated in more positive terms. The chaotic disorder present in so much of *El acoso,* from the background descriptions of the city to the narrative arrangement (in appearance at least), conveys wholly negative symbolism, which is heavily underlined by the strict order implicit in both the symphony and the liturgy. Here, too, in chapter 1, we find order collapsing into chaos. But chaos is now seen as including the potential for a new order. That is, whereas *El acoso* describes a situation whose positive resolution is possible, but remains excluded from the pattern of the narrative (we do not see whether any of the terrorist's comrades remain faithful to their ideals or whether the official Communist party line is having any useful consequences), *El siglo de las luces* includes an implicit resolution that is developed in *El recurso del método* and *La consagración de la primavera.*

In contrast to the complex narrative technique of *El acoso, El siglo de las luces* is told in a linear, chronological fashion, almost exclusively by an omniscient narrator. The only change of viewpoint arises from the fact that, after the opening, the narrative follows the fortunes first of Esteban and then of Sofía. The story is thus told from the angles of each in turn until the end, when Carlos pieces together the events of their last weeks. Thus up to a point the angle of vision rotates, but we never really get "inside" the characters in the way we do with the first-person narrator of *Los pasos perdidos*. The consequence is a certain loss of psychological depth and human ambiguity. The characters are cut to a pattern. Hugues, around whom Esteban and Sofía gravitate, and whose activities provide the main forward thrust of the plot, represents the corruption of the revolutionary ideal. Esteban, whose birthday interestingly coincides with Carpentier's and who, like him, is an asthmatic, plays the part of the passive, critical onlooker. Near the end he feels the same "weariness" with the constant ebb and flow of historical change without visible progress that afflicted Ti Noel at the end of *El reino de este mundo*. Sofía, on the other hand, expresses what Carpentier had abruptly proclaimed in the last pages of his second novel: that man must shoulder the burden of historical change and attempt to struggle forward despite all setbacks and despite his inability to see who will, or may, benefit. However much we identify with the three main characters on first reading the novel, when we stand back from the experience we realize that their evolution is subordinated to the plot and this in turn is tightly governed by the theme.

In the sort of fiction that rises above the level of mere entertainment, theme is what imposes direction on the events of the story (i.e., provides the criterion of selection) and, to the extent that the events and the characters involved in them are closely related, affects the roles of the latter. Even symbolism of the type common in *El siglo de las luces*, where, as elsewhere, its function is to carry part of the commentary, is conditioned by the basic theme. The problem here is not exclusively how we interpret that theme—that is, in terms of whether Carpentier saw historical change as a circular or as a spiral process. Another aspect is whether the theme itself, however we ultimately interpret it, constricts the way the novel is written and, in this case, the way the characters develop. Specifically: is there not something a trifle mechanical about the way Hugues's character develops around the same sort of "fissure" referred to in *El acoso:* upward (with reservations about his ideological extremism) and in tolerably good faith until he begins to organize privateering at the end of chapter 2; then downward into cynicism, self-interest, and racist tyranny, until Sofía leaves him in disgust? The rather similar evolution of Esteban from revolutionary fervor in the Paris of 1792 to complete disillusionment at the end of his stay with Hugues in Guadeloupe, reflects again this unambiguous treatment of character, which is rounded off by the transition to Sofía's renewed political enthusiasm just as that of the other two has collapsed. The pattern is unsubtle. The respective parabolas of Hugues and Esteban are too regular, while the death of Sofía's husband, which releases her to take up where Esteban had left off, is too convenient. It is all more tidy than life or human behavior tends to be. The cause is Carpentier's overanxiety to press home the theme.

A technically effective feature of Hugues's character-presentation is the suggestion from the outset that he is unstable. We note that his initial motive for visiting the family is part of an elaborate subterfuge: he is in fact organizing a subversive masonic network in the colony. But even before this is revealed, the first description of his appearance in subsection 4 of chapter 1 develops through a well-orchestrated set of dualities: "unalterability/mobility," "tension/ironic passivity," "laughter/a harsh and willful expression," "attraction/aversion," "ceremonious courtesy/discourtesy." These continue in the representation of Hugues in subsection 6: "vulgarity/distinction," "southern loquacity/economy of words." We read that various individuals seem lodged in his person; but in fact there are only two: the Jacobin extremist infatuated with Robespierre and the cynical opportunist. Even as he strikes the pose of the man whose "life was spent in the service of a dangerous conviction" (60), he is enriching himself by smuggling, while justifying it as fighting tyranny.

His first shift of allegiance comes early, when he disowns Freemasonry, and his first sign of weakness of personality, when he models himself consciously on his idol, Robespierre. But for the moment his energy prevails over adverse circumstances. Only when he has driven the enemy from Guadeloupe and established a revolutionary government there does he reveal that he possesses a "vigorous and energetic mind, but one so absolutely politicized that it refused to examine facts critically" (126). From then on he sinks into bloodthirsty dictatorship, greedy privateering, and slaving. By the end of chapter 3 he has relinquished all convictions, and when we meet him again in Cayenne he has thrown his weight behind what Sofía instantly recognizes as "a contemptible and cruel enterprise" (279). Behind his apparent energy there is in fact a certain passivity, a tendency to give way to events, until at last he is forced to recognize that he has been "carried along by others" (283) from the beginning and has played so many roles that he has lost his own identity and convictions.

Hugues, therefore, and to a lesser extent Billaud-Varennes, who begins as an intransigent libertarian in the Paris Revolutionary Assembly and ends as a slaveowner, represent at different levels the confusion and corruption of revolutionary ideals. A Marxist critic would probably add that they illustrate the fact that the French Revolution was in any case a "bourgeois" revolution, not supported by a systematic and "correct" ideology. It is significant that both the terrorist in *El acoso* and Hugues are shown as lacking sound ideological convictions, which they attempt to replace with extremist behavior. The pattern emerges again in the rival opposition party to that of the Student in *El recurso del método*. The role of Esteban is to supply the critical examination, which Hugues is so conspicuously unable to bring to bear. In addition the treatment of his character raises again the vexing question of Carpentier's attitude toward religion. Hugues, as befits so radical an opponent of the old regime, is not only irreligious but antireligious until he finds it opportune to reestablish Catholicism in his tiny dominion. His friend Ogé, on the other hand, recognizes (as Carpentier appears to do) that "man has always revealed a tenacious aspiration toward what might be called 'imitation of Christ' " (65), for which room must be found in revolutionary ideology.

The problem of harmonizing man's spiritual nature with revolutionary progress runs through the text, but centers principally on Esteban. In contrast to Hugues, he is a contemplative, unheroic figure who, despite his personal lack of religious convictions, is able to perceive the greater realism of Ogé's standpoint. Though infected in Paris by the fervor of the early days of the Revolution, he instinctively perceives it in terms of a stage in the spiritual pilgrimage of man toward dominion over his more selfish and violent instincts. When these instincts prevail during the Terror, he begins to see the contradictions of the revolutionary process and the threat it posed to those who dared to dissent, even in the name of revolutionary ideals themselves. But it is only on the voyage to Guadeloupe with Hugues in 1793 that his true critical propensities awaken. Thereafter his disenchantment grows in proportion to his double realization, first that the spirit of the people is out of accord with the revolutionary process set in motion on the island by Hugues, and second that despite the latter's brave words about "we, those without crosses, without redeemers, without God" (109) and his attacks on the clergy, religion proves impossible to extirpate. Sym-

bolically, during a storm at sea, Esteban instinctively crosses himself;
just as later Sofía, who has abandoned religion, instinctively uses
the traditional religious phrase "Dios te oiga" (May God hear you)
during her husband's last illness.

Since the characterization in *El siglo de las luces* is essentially
ideological and representative, the evolution of Esteban, apart from
his growing emotional involvement with Sofía, must be seen in
terms of his approach to a series of conscious conclusions about the
revolutionary epoch through which he lives. What are they? First
that revolutionary effort is founded on faith. The revolutionaries
"yearn for the Crucifix" (171). "The weakness of the Revolution,
which deafened the ears of the world so much with the voices of a
new *Dies Irae,*" he reflects, "lies in its lack of valid gods" (191).
This aspect of the novel has been cogently analyzed by Claude
Dumas.[5] Second, that the terrible cost of the revolution has to be
measured in human sacrifice not only of those whose lives the revolution devours, but also of those who suffer a "change of soul" and
are morally destroyed by the experience. Third, that the "Promised
Land" of the revolution is a mere phrase, nothing but words, and
that any such better world exists potentially only inside each individual, not in the collectivity.

Critics, like Morón,[6] who regard Carpentier at this stage as an
antirevolutionary writer have fallen into the trap of identifying Carpentier's own ideas too readily with these conclusions of Esteban's.
But not only do they not reveal Esteban's whole outlook, they are
even less representative of his creator's. That this is the case is
suggested by his later comment:

Esteban has a terrible defect and it is that he is the utopian thinker, the
idealist who really has not got a political sense or conscience. . . . [He
is] . . . an intellectual who constructs a preconceived idea of what a
revolution ought to be, or the revolution, or his revolution if it is that of
his own country, and who, as soon as the revolution fails to fit in with
the preconceived patterns, preestablished by him, and follows its own
course, being inflexible, unable to follow the zig-zag line of events, begins
to lose his balance, begins to be irritated, begins not to understand what
is going on and ends by denying to some extent what was his ideal. This
character we have seen multiplied by a hundred . . . in countries all over
the world since the beginning of the century. That is, the intellectual who
embraces a pattern.[7]

Near the middle of the novel Esteban undergoes two important experiences, one while climbing a tree in Guadeloupe and the other while contemplating a shell during a privateering trip. In each case he is made deeply aware of an ongoing process of natural evolution. The end of the second experience is not a conclusion but a question: "What must there be around me which is already defined, inscribed, present, and which I cannot as yet understand? What sign, what message, what warning, in the curls of the chicory plant, the alphabet of the mosses, the geometry of the rose-apple? To gaze at a shell. Just one. Te Deum" (155). The process of decay and resurrection that Esteban notices around the tree and the Spiral (significantly capitalized) he perceives in the shell belie his more pessimistic conclusions and express rather more what Carpentier himself appears to believe. Labanyi writes: "The natural process of decay is used as a symbolic pointer to the necessary corruption inherent in any revolutionary process. . . . But . . . decay and destruction are the necessary prerequisites of life and rebirth . . . the emphasis shifts from death to resurrection . . . corruption of the revolutionary ideal is a necessary stage in the germination of a new idealism."[8]

This view seems to have become more pronounced as Carpentier grew older. But in essence it was always there, latent, in the part of his mind that, through sundry compromises, never completely abandoned the political aspirations that led to his imprisonment in 1923, his support for the Spanish Republic and for the Venezuelan Communist party during the 1940s and 1950s. Another important feature of the question is raised by Esteban's reflection that "something had to be done that would give a meaning to his existence" (111). Hugues remarks later that "the revolution has given an object to my existence" (126). Later still Sofía, Carlos, and Jorge insist that "it was necessary to be aware of one's epoch, to have an object in life" (225). Even of the minor and prematurely disillusioned Martínez de Ballesteros it is said that "he would go on seeking a reason for living—for surviving—lending his services to a revolution totally different from that which had set aflame his first enthusiasms" (138). The insistent repetition of this idea proclaims Carpentier's belief that there is a quasi-metaphysical force, of a piece with man's inextinguishable longing to imitate Christ, which will always drive him to try to fulfill, however disastrously, an ideal of radical social change. Esteban has another vision of this as his ship passes the mouth of the Orinoco in subsection 34.

The irrepressible survival of this force (which Carpentier would clearly have liked to see channeled away from religion toward the kingdom of this world) is expressed in the novel by the upsurge of rebelliousness in Sofía just as Esteban has lapsed into pessimism and the ("bourgeois") ideal of individual salvation. "Sofía is the absolute contrary [of Esteban",] Carpentier was to write. "Sofía is praxis. Sofía is the woman who feels instinctively what has to be done and which way one should go. Unhappily it is not given to her to live in a moment when she could give the full measure of herself."[9] Sofía begins life in the novel as a conventional, convent-educated girl, made uneasy by references to sexuality or by disrespect toward the Church. Hugues's desire for her, however, coinciding with a symbolic cyclone, brings disorder into the hitherto imposed order of her life, and with it a new self-awareness. The shift in her outlook finds expression in physical terms during her first sea voyage, when all her senses come to life and she allows Hugues to become her lover.

In contrast to *El acoso*, where sexuality is associated with betrayal, here both in Esteban and Sofía it is part of a process of liberation. Ironically, too, it is Hugues who releases the process in the two cousins. When Sofía (whose name, the author reminds us, means "Happy Wisdom") reappears in chapter 5, the process of transformation of her life, to which she had submitted at the beginning of the novel, has been restrained by her marriage into a rich, slave-owning family. But Esteban's earlier translations of revolutionary pamphlets (which he now disowns) have done their work in providing a focal point for the longing for social betterment that Carpentier presents as ineradicable.

The death of her husband, who, like her father, had symbolized order and tradition while, in his case, paying lip-service to the ideals of liberty and social change, marks the end of a second epoch in Sofía's life. Once more the meal brought in from a hotel after the funeral signifies the beginning of a new phase of transformation, which, like the first, leads her to Hugues and to what she believes will be "an epic world inhabited by titans" (247). Meanwhile Carpentier, the master ironist, who has used Esteban's now disowned translations to excite his cousin's revolutionary enthusiasm, causes Esteban to feign renewed belief in their doctrines in order to protect her flight. In Cayenne Sofía's illusions of lending herself to an epic struggle in which "her life, at last, had a course and a meaning"

(268) last even less time than Esteban's had in France. Paternalism, moderation, and above all the reestablishment of slavery convince her that "she was present at the gradual reestablishment of all that seemed to have been abolished" (274). But, unlike Esteban, she finds the experience of disillusionment salutary: it teaches her what to reject. Abandoning Hugues and with him compromises in general, she proudly assumes her sexual and personal liberty and sails for Spain. There she achieves the release of Esteban and, brushing aside his now preromantic sentimentalizations, drags him once more into the revolutionary struggle in which both die anonymously.

It is unimportant that 1808 in Spain was the prelude to a century and a half of turmoil and tyranny, just as it is unimportant that Hugues's revolutionary regime in Guadeloupe collapsed in blood, greed, and superstition. What matters, as the book's epigraph proclaims, is that words ("Liberty," "Progress," "The Promised Land," and so on) are not spoken in vain. Willy-nilly, Hugues, Esteban, and Sofía all experience man's instinctive urge to press for change, and all contribute, even as they betray and disown it, to the painfully slow, hideously costly process of social transformation.

El acoso was basically an "interrogative" novel. Both in form and content it asked questions about political behavior (and about human destiny), as well as about the nature of reality. *El siglo de las luces* is a much more "declaratory" novel. Its form, instead of being strange and disturbing, is relatively conventional. The straight, chronological account of events, with logical articulations and a familiar approach to characterization, appeals directly to the reader's will to believe that the world is meaningful and explicable, that reality is comfortable and comprehensible. The narrative method, that is, provides an implicitly reassuring framework, within which Carpentier can suggest the interpretation of historical change we have attempted to clarify. A short way to define many novels is to say that they contain a series of happenings together with a commentary. In the case of *El siglo de las luces,* which is so heavily geared toward interpretation, the commentary is rather intrusive and is carried in several different ways. Since any serious plot implies a vision of reality, plot structure itself can be seen as an indirect form of commentary. Thus when we consider that of *El siglo de las luces* we have to look both at how it functions as a story and at how it puts forth Carpentier's outlook.

A feature of the storyline is the way in which it is spurred on at intervals by sudden arbitrary events rather than by decisions on the part of the characters. What triggers the opening situation is the unexpected death of the old merchant, followed by the unannounced visit of Hugues. Once he has exerted his fascination, a cyclone and the discovery of his subversive activities lead Esteban and Sofía to flee with him. The burning of Port-au-Prince in turn leads to the precipitate decision of Hugues and Esteban to sail for France. Similarly, after Esteban's return to Havana, the death of Sofía's husband in an epidemic releases her to join Hugues in Cayenne, where a further epidemic surrounds the end of their relationship. In the last episode a sudden rebellion in Madrid provides the scenario for Sofía and Esteban's death in the cause of liberty. Given that the plot follows the fortunes, not so much of Hugues, who is hyperactive, but of Esteban, a timid, contemplative personality, and of Sofía, who as a woman, cannot readily influence events, these successive turns of fortune serve to maintain the tempo of the narrative. But they can also be seen as a deliberately introduced series of cataclysms destructive of the old order, that is, as functional in relation to the theme. The other way in which the plot reveals Carpentier's ideological stance is through the manner in which the happenings are selected and arranged. This operates so as to provide an ironic contrast to the ideals from which the events spring. Except for Hugues's brief campaign against the British, examples of heroism, magnanimity, and disinterested effort are excluded. Even Hugues's military success is later caricatured in his catastrophic campaign against the rebellious blacks in Cayenne. Meanwhile the circumstances of Sofía's release from the constraints of marriage in order to join in what she believes will be revolutionary endeavor and Esteban's reassertion of his revolutionary ideals in order to cover her escape are managed in such a way as to express the constant rebirth of "faith" (in the establishment of a more just kingdom of this world) out of defeat and disillusionment.

Within this general scheme we must once more examine the opening, almost always Carpentier's strong point. The novel begins with a first-person mental reflection by Esteban as he contemplates the guillotine on the bow of the ship taking Hugues and himself to the Caribbean. It introduces symbolically an aspect of the theme: the price in terror and death exacted by radical social change. But at the same time the frame of the guillotine is a door through which the stars and the "road" of the Milky Way can be seen: an opening through which we can glimpse the ideal. The first chapter is full of foreshadowing technique. It is patterned so as to establish the shape of the rest of the narrative. The death of the old merchant and the cyclone imply the end of the old traditional social order. There is an interval of disorder, free fantasy, and chaotic liberty before Hugues arrives with ideas that portend a new reality based on revolutionary order. The executor and the authorities who unmask and pursue Hugues and Ogé represent the countervailing forces of greed and repression. The symbolic importance of this chapter is underlined when Esteban returns to find Carlos occupying his father's position, with a portrait of the old man presiding over the firm, and all much as it had been. Jorge's death and the meal that follows are a pointed remake of the situation in chapter 1 and set going a second cycle of events, centered on Sofía.

In the center of the novel the political evolution of Guadeloupe, imposed by Hugues, mimicks that of France, but with a time-lag imposed by distance that turns the revolutionary process on the island into an ironic mockery of that taking place in the mother country. Essentially, however, the middle and later sections of the novel are committed to an effect of reduplication, as Sofía's experiences in Cayenne reemphasize those of Esteban in Guadeloupe, but in a different way. Finally we must notice the shift in the last chapter—the epilogue—from predominantly confident, third-person, omniscient narration[10] to the less certain account of the last days of Sofía and Esteban pieced together from hearsay by Carlos. Plainly, Carpentier's object in adopting this technique for the last few pages of the novel is to avoid questions of motivation. The last episodes are narrated as seen by strangers who can only offer a version of the facts, with no explanation. Thus the reader is left to consider for himself the possible causes, motives, and even the significance of the two young people's action, based on his assessment of the preceding narrative. So the plot is in a sense open-ended. One can interpret Sofía and Esteban's act as a piece of folly, in view of their joint earlier disillusionment; as futile, in view of the subsequent events in Spain; or alternatively as an expression of the inevitability with which revolutionary action is reborn time after time.

It is hardly necessary to stress the use Carpentier makes of the characters for the purposes of commentary, given that all the major ones are either representative or intelligent and articulate onlookers.

Just as the old merchant, Sofía's father, represents the traditionalism of the Spanish ascendency, masked by claptrap, and Jorge, her husband, represents the planter aristocracy with naive pretensions to libertarian ideals, so Carlos, her brother, represents the native-born bourgeoisie, which, for its own benefit, was to push aside Spanish dominion over Cuba. The novel begins and ends, not with Esteban, Sofía, or Hugues, but with Carlos. In this way Carpentier reminds us that the historical process he is describing, though revolutionary, was in the end going to benefit the middle class. Mocega-González's view that Carlos represents mankind in general carries little conviction.[11] Carpentier himself has written: "So far as Carlos is concerned, he is simply the kind of man who is endowed with an ideal. We have seen plenty of them—he is the least interesting character in the novel—in whom the ideal does not outlast his reaching twenty-five or twenty-six, when the need to make a living, to look after his business, bourgeoisify him."[12]

Esteban and Sofía serve to vitalize the narrative viewpoint, which often abandons the detached, omniscient tone and uses their eyes and reactions to present a close-up of events. Their moment of awareness and their specific comments signal to the reader appropriate responses, although, particularly in the case of Esteban, they are not always unambiguous. Less commonly, the narrator intervenes to comment via a minor character such as Martínez de Ballesteros, Brohier, or Sieger, created largely for the purpose, or else comments directly, as in the last sentence of chapter 2, which maliciously records the survival of the shopkeeper in the tyrant of Guadeloupe.

Probably the most interesting aspect of the commentary is to be found in the symbolism, dominated by the picture of an explosion in a Cathedral by François Nomé (Monsú Desiderio), an actual picture currently in the Fitzwilliam Museum, Cambridge. The last sentence of the novel asserts enigmatically that as Carlos closes the door of the mansion in Madrid from which Sofía and Esteban had gone out to their deaths, the picture "ceased to have a subject," thus identifying it with the novel as a whole. If that is so, its meaning is that of the novel also. The cathedral stands primarily for the old, traditional, theocentric view of life and society, which (especially in the Spanish-speaking world) the principles of the French Revolution blasted apart. But not totally; a considerable part of the edifice remains standing. The symbolism here corresponds to all those aspects of the novel: the regular reemergence of the Church, the survival of oppression and slavery, the "longing for the Crucifix" of the revolutionaries (in the sense of their desire to give life some transcendental meaning), and the survival of the bourgeoisie, which run counter to the book's revolutionary ideology. On the other hand, the part of the cathedral that has been blown up is not seen in ruins on the ground but in the act of falling, "perpetual fall without falling," as the text puts it. In other words, the revolution is always in the act of destroying; we never see the completed process, much less the rebuilding of another cathedral dedicated not to God but to man and to the kingdom of this world (i.e., a completely revolutionized society). Esteban interprets the picture as relating possibly to his own being, to his times, and to the Christian Church, all ravaged by the revolution but not totally shattered. His act of throwing a stool at the picture symbolizes his disgust with revolutionary outbursts, which, in the nature of things, can never wholly destroy or totally create afresh. But this should not be taken to reflect Carpentier's disgust. Part of the message of the book is that we must not expect too much from revolutionary endeavor, either in terms of human or social change, but neither must we abandon or try to obstruct the endeavor itself, since it expresses something profound in man's makeup. Some readers may find it a pity that Carpentier modified this message in *La consagración de la primavera*.

Apart from the references to the picture, the rest of the novel contains, in Labanyi's words, "a multiple network of symbolic references."[13] The family mansion in Havana, as Ortega points out,[14] stands like one of the poles in the novel, representing the continuity of bourgeois commerce and stability. Nothing revolutionary happens inside it, and it resists the symbolic cyclone that marks a turning point in the lives of Esteban and Sofía. Claude Dumas[15] has emphasized the symbolism of the episode in which Esteban contemplates the Crucifix facing the sea: Creation facing Evolution. The migration of the Caribs toward the sea clearly symbolizes man's unending quest for a Promised Land, which Esteban and Sofía in turn seek through revolution. The dual nature of revolutionary activity is symbolized by the juxtaposition of the guillotine and the printing press on the ship sailing to Guadeloupe. The shape of the shell that Esteban contemplates stands for the possibly spiral course of history. The herd of swine invading Hugues's house in Cayenne is an allegory of the contamination of the ideal Sofía still attributes to her lover. The tomb of the last Byzantine emperor, which Sofía visits, is, in a Caribbean and revolutionary context, an ironic symbol of the tenacious survival of the past in unexpected ways and places. In his interview with Claude Fell in 1965 Carpentier emphasized his use of red as a symbolic color. Finally the forces or resistance of nature: the cyclone, the storm at sea, the plagues, the forest that Hugues cannot tame, all symbolize the disorderly nature of reality, which the uncompromising pseudorationality of French (or any) revolutionary dogma cannot overcome. All these examples show the importance of symbolic commentary in the narrative strategy of this novel.

For many readers *Los pasos perdidos* and *El siglo de las luces* are Carpentier's most memorable novels. But the former points backward toward a refuge and an origin that offer the illusion of an escape from man's Sisyphus-like "Task." *El siglo de las luces* points forward toward ever new, but ever ambiguous, attempts on man's part to strike a balance between utopian aspirations and historical conditions. To that extent we may agree with King that it is wrong to suggest that the novel condemns revolutionary effort. What it offers is a warning from Caribbean history. Despite his modification of it in the light of his post-1959 Cuban experience, that warning remains Carpentier's most mature expression of his personal insight.

Chapter Seven
Reasons of State
Return to Cuba

As we saw earlier, after nearly six years in pre-Castro Cuba, Carpentier had moved in 1945 to Caracas, where, apart from journalism, teaching History of Culture at the School of Plastic Arts, and working in commercial radio and television, he completed *El reino de este mundo* and wrote *Los pasos perdidos, El acoso* and most of *El siglo de las luces* as well as some short stories. He stayed happily in Caracas for fourteen years. But in 1959 the news of Fidel Castro's triumphant entry into Havana broke over Latin America. Carpentier has given a fictionalized account of the reaction in Caracas in a piece written in 1964, later incorporated into *La consagración de la primavera*. After a brief trip to Cuba, finding himself welcomed by the new regime, which he strongly supported, he and his wife returned to Havana in July 1959, He was placed in charge of the National Publishing House, later the Book Institute, which has the monopoly of publishing in Cuba. Also, while his wife participated actively in the campaign against illiteracy, he returned to teaching History of Culture at Havana University. Speaking in 1975, back briefly in Caracas, he explained: "I heard the voices that had begun to sound out afresh, taking me back to my adolescense; I listened to the new voices that now sounded out, and I believed it my duty to place my energies, my abilities—if I had any—at the service of the great Latin American historical task that was being carried out in my country." He added: "At that moment we all had the sensation that we could be useful. It is what I have called in a speech, to get out of the period of solitude, to enter the stage of solidarity."[1]

Carpentier joined the revolutionary regime, according to his own statement, "following a long personal tradition."[2] All was not plain sailing, however. Despite his claim that writers and artists in Castro's Cuba were free to create in any way that was not antirevolutionary, the evidence points in the other direction. Certainly when Carpentier returned to Cuba he was arguably in a rather ambiguous relationship with what was to crystallize into a semiofficial attitude toward literature. The emphasis in his work (especially in the as yet unpublished *El siglo de las luces*) on the difficulties and contradictions of revolutionary activity and his complex vision of man's onward march in time, did not endear him in the long run to an intelligentsia who wished to see literature harnessed afresh to what a spokesman, Portuondo, called "its old social function, its duty of immediate service."[3] Judith Weiss comments: "The intellectual elite has only one real alternative in this situation: to subordinate personal needs to the demands of the revolution; to participate in the raising of consciousness"; at the expense, that is, of "the idea of intellectual freedom as professed by a bourgeois society."[4]

Although he contributed to *Casa de las Américas* and served on one of its occasional prize-giving committees, Carpentier does not appear to have been wholly accepted by the editorial group of that immensely influential magazine. Though he authorized a reedition of *Ecue-Yamba-O* in Cuba in 1967, he continued to publish his new works in Mexico and Spain (perhaps for copyright reasons). It is likely to be some time before it becomes clear why he gave up his editorial work and joined the Cuban embassy in Paris as cultural attaché, but in the late 1960s and early 1970s he is thought to have fallen to some extent into disgrace. It is anybody's guess how far the cultural atmosphere in Cuba may have affected some of his declarations about literature and about his own work. Be that as it may, his seventieth birthday in 1974 was the occasion for official celebrations followed by an honorary doctorate of the University of Havana. The publication of the very strongly pro-Castro *La consagración de la primavera* in 1978 removed any lingering doubts about his orthodoxy and at the time of his death he was accepted as one of the grand old men of Cuban letters.

El recurso del método

In an interview in 1976 Carpentier said: "The Latin American dictator is such a characteristic product of [Latin] American soil that it is necessary to show his reality and try to explain in depth the enigma of his periodic and almost continuous reappearance on the Latin American scene."[5] The key expression here is the phrase "explain in depth" *(desentrañar)*. Something like a hundred novels have been written about dictatorship in Latin America. But what characterizes most of them is that they do not try to explain it, but merely describe it, usually in horrendous terms. Such literature of simple protest is currently somewhat out of fashion (except in Cuba) since the youthful readership needs no sensitizing and the middle and upper classes enjoy seeing themselves and their leaders pilloried, granting prizes and other awards to their critics while taking care to ignore what they say. A fair number of young protest writers tend to make their peace with presidential regimes as they get older. Carpentier's situation is interesting.

After initially including crude protest elements in *Ecue-Yamba-O*, he veered away from them toward less obviously "committed" fiction with a dismissive remark in the prologue to *El reino de este mundo* about "the commonplaces of the committed writer." *El acoso* can be read in one sense as anti-committed in that it contains, though from an orthodox Party standpoint, a critique of direct action by small groups. Again, the minor revolution the narrator of *Los pasos perdidos* witnesses on his way to the jungle is presented condescendingly as rather anachronistic, part of the journey into the past. But with Hugues in *El siglo de las luces,* the cruelty, the greedy ambition and the lack of political principles, typical of hunger for power surface again alongside the theme of the betrayal of true revolutionary effort.

Hugues prefigures aspects of the dictator in *El recurso del método,* but there are important differences. At first Hugues is an ideologue, intoxicated with new subversive doctrines. Only later does he turn into an unscrupulous opportunist and almost to the end enjoys a certain grandeur of personality. This is partly because he is seen from the outside, from the viewpoints of Esteban and Sofía. The "First Magistrate," on the other hand, is seen partly from the inside, in the first person, and is revealed as utterly unscrupulous from the outset. We learn that near the beginning of his political career he at first fought for a particular regime only to overthrow it later, just as Galván and Hoffmann, his adversaries, try to do. He has no genuine convictions at all and his regime staggers along without any fixed ideology. This is the story of the maturity and decline of a shrewd and cynical political improviser in the early part of this century, a dictator who shifts nimbly from one stance to another and uses whichever means seem most likely to succeed in the struggle to cling to power. The plot deals with his triumph over two rebellions, the plenitude of his regime during the First World War, and its collapse in the 1920s after the appearance of a left-wing opponent, the Student. The scene alternates between an imaginary Latin American state and Paris, where the dictator and his family enjoy long periods of residence.

Having come to power through a coup, he retains it by the classic methods of fixing elections and altering the Constitution. Bribery, a fraudulent referendum, police terror, racist rhetoric, and above all the support of the United States government are all enlisted to maintain his position. His motto is unequivocal: "in politics, what counts is success."[6] Hence the Spanish title of the novel. The "method" refers to the repertoire of tricks and sometimes violent expedients by which Latin American dictators keep themselves in power. The novel is largely dedicated to unmasking the way the "method" works and what is effective against it. About the alternative we must be rather careful. At an early point in the novel the suggestion is slyly introduced that the "method" of the dictator contrasts with the "Cartesian spirit" of France. To the unwary reader the implication is that part of the ills of Latin America will be cured when the rickety improvisations of its dictatorial regimes are replaced with more rationally conceived institutions such as those of France. But we do not need to recall *El siglo de las luces* to remember that France is the homeland of a failed revolution, taken over by bourgeois moderates in their own interest. Nor do we need to look too closely at the France of the early decades of this century to see that France is hardly the ideal model for Latin American states to follow. In fact, Peralta, the dictator's secretary, reminds a patronizing French academician that his country's record of oppression, massacres, and civil strife stretches from the Albigensians to the Paris Commune.

To those critics who perceive Carpentier's thought as negative and pessimistic, the conclusion is obvious. If Europe can offer no better alternatives, Latin America will continue to produce dictatorial regimes in an unceasing Eternal Return. Equally, governments, whether in Europe or Latin America, will continue to oppress, massacre, and deceive. This is a possible meaning of *El recurso del método,* though one that Carpentier has specifically repudiated. It can be supported by an appeal to prominent aspects of the novel's technique. The perhaps symbolic mirror before which the interview between the Student and the dictator takes place may imply that the latter—who recognizes his own youthful illusions in those of the Student—merely reflects the future role of the young agitator. Similarly the repetitions cunningly intercalated into the text, such as the references to the alarm clock and to Drag Day, together with the implicit comparisons between events in Europe, such as the Great War and the Depression, and similar events in the dictator's state, can be read as implying a futile, circular Human Condition. In chapter 8 the dictator sees himself trapped in a magic circle traced by the devil: "History, which was his own, since he played a part in it, was history that repeated itself, that chased its own tail, that swallowed itself up, that came to a halt each time. . . . Time stopped in a military coup, curfew, suspension of constitutional guarantees, reestablishment of normality and words, words, words . . . " (152). Hence Vich-Campos's remark: "Reality seems to have got stuck in a mechanical repetition, a systematic succession of dictators. The novel, then, is deeply pessimistic, particularly if one thinks of the whole of Carpentier's reflections on absolute power. And the humour does not modify this pessimism, quite the contrary."[7]

And yet it is noteworthy that, for example, Mocega-González,[8] in her anxiety to prove that the Student will turn inevitably into a remake of the dictator, avoids any reference to the Student's role after he has been interviewed by the latter, or to Carpentier's own remark that the Student is "the man who does not accept that state of affairs and advances toward the future."[9] Carpentier's affirmations after his return to Cuba about the meaning of his work are sometimes disingenuous and sometimes downright misleading, but here his statement accords perfectly with the text itself. The American consul, for instance, who can be taken as an impartial observer, asserts that the Student is "a man of a new race inside his own race" (338). Subsequently we meet the young man on his way to an International Congress to oppose colonialism and imperialism. His companions are Nehru, the architect of India's independence, and Mella, co-founder of the Cuban Communist party. Unless one is prepared to interpret this scene as implying that Carpentier had ironically in mind the hundreds of thousands of deaths that accompanied Indian independence and the executions ordered by Castro (which is possible, but improbable), one must conclude that his references to time's "marking time," as it were, relate to dictatorial Latin America and to capitalistic Europe; for both Nehru and Mella portend change. We must also note Carpentier's insistence that "if I thought that the abominable dictatorships that today, in this century, are borne by many countries of our continent, constituted an endemic disease, imposed by fate on Latin America, inseparable from our continental destiny, I should repudiate my Latin American birth."[10]

The Student, then, seems to be presented as a precursor of Castro's Communist regime, seen as the way to break out of the circle of immobilistic repetition. This is confirmed by *La consagración de la primavera*. Further confirmation is provided by the dictator himself. As Dorfman emphasizes,[11] he is constantly being overtaken by change he cannot understand. A function of the references to his old-fashioned tastes in art is to emphasize that he belongs to the past. Thus, when a revolution (which, however distorted in its effects, is intended to portend "the" revolution) deposes him, he returns to Paris to find his old conventional pictures and sculptures replaced by Picassos and Légers. The relationship between the progress of art and that of society was to become prominent in Carpentier's next two novels also.

El recurso del método is set in the period between 1913, with the dictator already firmly in power, and his fall around 1927. The archetypal central figure is built up from stock characteristics and others borrowed from Machado and Batista of Cuba, Pérez Jiménez of Venezuela, Rojas Pinilla of Colombia, and Tinoco of Costa Rica. That is, he represents dictatorship not merely before Castro's rise to power seemed to have altered the situation, but even before Marxism had made a really effective penetration into Latin America. We are dealing with a figure who is already an anachronism. It is not that his artistic and literary tastes alone are out of date; his mental model of the progress of society is all wrong. Despite his awareness (which is part of the genuine complexity of his character presentation) that the Cartesian rationalism he has been taught to associate with France is not really characteristic of that country's historical development or way of life, nor is it remotely applicable to Latin America, he himself remains obstinately Cartesian: "resolved, by Cartesian custom to take as certain whatever struck him as self-evidently true" (131). Like the narrator of *Los pasos perdidos* in the jungle, he is vainly seeking in France an illusory lost origin, in this case for his regime and outlook. His returns to Europe can be seen as repeated attempts to "return to the source." He continues to try to develop his state along "modern" European lines, though the result is a parody. For at that time Europe itself was moving

away from order, convention, and rationalism. Dialectical reasoning
was beginning to challenge Cartesianism and the Russian Revolution
had shattered the stable pattern of European society to which the
dictator clings.

Nonetheless, as Carpentier himself has pointed out,[12] the dictator
is, up to a point, enlightened. He is neither a semiliterate boor nor
a mediocrity, but a man with some pretensions to culture and
progressive ideas as long as they do not interfere with his personal
power. Unlike Asturias in *El Señor Presidente,* Carpentier is not
primarily concerned to evoke horror and disgust in the reader. His
aim is to provoke amused contempt by means of caricature. The
dictator is not a bloody-handed ogre, but a sometimes attractive
scoundrel. But he is not an antihero: one who betrays a better nature
through wrong choices and with guilt feelings. He is a cynic and
a hypocrite, a fake, who knows he is acting a part. But he glories
in it and acts it entertainingly, even to the point of making fun of
himself, until someone or something threatens to take the role away.
Then he shows his teeth.

As with Ricardo in "El derecho de asilo" Carpentier has a problem.
He has to induce us to be interested in and amused by the dictator,
without our liking him or sympathizing with him too much, while
at the same time allowing the humor to develop into irony and
sarcasm as the serious implications of having such a man in power
are explored. To achieve this Carpentier exploits the difference between the dictator in private life and the public figure. The alter-
nations between Paris and Latin America as settings provide an extra
bonus, since it is chiefly in Paris that we see the dictator in his
intimacy, while in Latin America he mainly plays his public role.

Once more the pattern is set in the opening chapter. We first
meet the dictator in a hammock in a house in Paris overlooking the
Arc de Triomphe. The hammock indicates his unbreakable attachment to his Latin American roots, re-emphasized at the end of the
novel. At a deeper level, the hammock, slung in a Parisian mansion,
symbolizes the irreconcilability of Latin America to Europeanization,
one of the basic themes here, just as it was in *El siglo de las luces.*
The Arc de Triomphe, like the eagle on the inkwell in the presidential palace and the souvenir of Waterloo, represents ironically
the dictator's suppressed Napoleonic ambitions, parodied in his
grotesque military campaigns and his corrupt, rickety administration, which has to be propped up by the United States.

In the first part of the chapter the man behind the facade presents himself. He is cynically conscious of his far-from-Napoleonic cowardice in battle; pleased with his night in a fancy brothel, but worried that it may have offended the Virgin, who is the protrectress of his country; vain of his presumed culture, but really interested in pornography; susceptible to the most fawning flattery; terrified of his grown-up daughter; in short, a harmless-seeming, even slightly comic figure, but nobody's fool. The first-person narration is crucial. We begin to warm to this human, down-to-earth figure, loving his creature comforts and preening himself in front of his tailor's mirror, but striking no pretentious attitudes. He seems the very reverse of a sinister tyrant. But the sudden announcement of a rebellion against his regime produces a dramatic change, marked by a highly tactical shift from first to third-person narration. The public figure takes over. He is still amusing up to a point: his flow of obscenities contrasts deliciously with the portentous tone of his message to the nation. But the dictator proper has replaced the bon vivant. Part of the national territory is to be traded to the United Fruit Company in return for arms; opponents are to be shot down; nothing is to interfere with the dictator's inalienable right to do as he pleases, despite constitutional guarantees.

The alternation between the not unattractive, self-indulgent but self-aware man and the sanguinary, utterly unscrupulous dictator persists until the "First Magistrate's" fall from power. It governs the presentation of the central figure and gives rise to the alternation of tones in the novel, more comic in France or at the New York opera, more serious and sarcastic in Latin America, which contrasts with the unrelieved horror of Asturias's *El Señor Presidente*. But it is not the novel's only structuring device. For the dictator must be seen as part of a system, and here too we see a clear pattern of alternation. Regimes in Latin America are apt to be brought down by military coups or else by sporadic civil disorder under the leadership of middle-class intellectuals. In the bulk of the narrative Carpentier suggests that neither method is effective. We can recognize in the first five chapters two basic cycles. The first comprises two military coups, which the dictator, with cynical barbarity, suppresses. Then, after an interlude of wartime prosperity, the second involves the growth of civilian opposition. This is of two kinds. One, based on terrorism and rhetoric, leads directly to a fresh dictatorship under the crank, Leoncio Martínez. The other, led by the

Student, aspires to be a genuinely popular uprising, adequately prepared, with sound Marxist principles and leadership. In this way Carpentier is able to set out the field of forces within which dictatorship in Latin America has traditionally operated, and also to indicate an alternative.

Why does Carpentier introduce two military rebellions? The answer must lie in the contrast between them. The deliberately comic similarities in the telegrams that announce their outbreak emphasize the inevitability of such coups in a country that, we are told, has already had fifty-three of them in a century. But thereafter the two rebellions are clearly differentiated. That of Galván is highly typical in that it contains both a military element, suppressed by the execution of its leader, and a civil element, led by Leoncio Martínez together with a group of French-trained junior officers. This is put down by bribery of the soldiers and massacre of the civilians. The characteristics of both the military and the civilian wings of this rebellion are tragicomic incompetence and mere impulsiveness. It symbolizes the folly of so many inadequately planned, futile, Latin American insurrections and is indeed condemned by the politically sophisticated students in the capital before the campaign against it begins. This, then, is how not to do it.

Hoffmann's abortive revolt is significant in a quite different way. Carpentier satirizes the dictator's instrumentalization of the myth of the spiritual superiority of the Latin race to defeat Hoffmann, even after he himself has become disillusioned with it because of his unpopularity in France after the massacres of the previous campaign. What matters in this case is less Hoffmann's revolt itself than the dictator's nimble modification of the "method" in order to deal with it and his success in carrying the people with him. Also Hoffmann's tin-pot rebellion parodies Germany's invasion of Belgium and France in 1914. We are intended to draw the conclusion that Europeans are hardly in a position to criticize Latin America's trifling conflicts, when they are responsible for struggles of the magnitude of World War I. Once more the two geographical dimensions of the novel, Europe and Latin America, are used to comment ironically on one another.

The central section of the novel takes up another aspect of the context of dictatorship in Latin America: dependency. If Carpentier's expositions reveal exceptional functionality, after *Los pasos perdidos* they tend to have very strong centers also. In the middle of *Los pasos perdidos* we reach Santa Mónica itself; in the middle of *El siglo de las luces* revolutionary activity degenerates into privateering; in the case of *El recurso del método* the apotheosis of the dictator's regime is shattered by the explosion of the first bomb. His career is broadly symmetrical: up to here he is generally successful; beyond this point his fortunes decline. Form in fiction matters either because it is functional or because it is meaningful; in Carpentier's best work it is usually both. The center of *El recurso del método* is functional in that it juxtaposes dramatically the apogee of the dictator's regime with the threat to its stability. It is meaningful in that the shift coincides with the end of export-based prosperity. It has nothing to do with the dictator's policies or lack of them, or with the efforts of his opponents. The real destinies of the country are not in his hands or theirs. They are in the hands of the great powers.

The shift comes in subchapter 12; now something new in the country emerges. It gradually destabilizes society and facilitates a change of regime. It is, predictably, the force of Communist-led subversion captained by the Student. The scene in which he and the dictator meet is in some ways the novel's ideological climax. But the Student and his movement do not succeed, for this is still only the 1920s. What triumphs is the Alpha-Omega party (non-ideological: all things to all men) of the crackpot Martínez with United States support. Meanwhile the narrative has bifurcated. On the one hand we follow the fortunes of the regime to their ironic climax in the opera season. On the other the countermethod confronting the "method" of the dictator reaches a climax in the General Strike, of the people as a whole. The self-deceit of the crumbling regime is aptly symbolized in the capitol building, a monument to nonexistent democracy, the Statue of the Republic, anachronistic and assembled out of bits and pieces, and the opera, a perfect simulacrum of the regime itself. But if the first of these is a bad imitation of that of Washington, the Model Prison is well in advance of its foreign counterparts. The one thing that Latin America could do really well in the 1920s (and later) was torture and oppress.

The last resources of the dictator's "method," the bombardment of the shops during the strike and his feigned death, climax in their utter grotesqueness all his earlier expedients. But the reader's interest has shifted to the opposition. As before, Carpentier condemns anarchoid direct action. The force he wishes to legitimize is that of the people, collective, systematic, and accompanied by increased political awareness. Ultimately it involves even the middle class, upon whom the dictator had formerly relied for passive support. The theme is developed in the evolution of the central couple of *La consagración de la primavera*. One reason why Carpentier set the novel in the period 1913–27 was because at this time Latin America began to exchange economic and cultural dependency on Europe for similar dependency on the United States. In contrast, Carpentier advocates true Latin Americanness and loyalty to popular roots. Meaningful in this connection, as Dorfman has indicated, [13] are Miguel Estatua and the American consul. While the dictator, like the three artists in *Los pasos perdidos*, is blind to the cultural potential of his own continent, Miguel extracts simple and beautiful statues from American rock. Later, he and the common people resist to the end, fighting both the dictator and his North American backers. Biblical terms and allusions alert us to analogies with Christ. The American consul is a man of Negro blood who is passing for white. Unlike the dictator, who has prospered by turning his back on his own mixed racial origins, he has borne discrimination in order to stay faithful to his background, symbolized in his collection of roots. The dictator partially rediscovers his Latin American identity in exile, but too late. The moment of his final physical collapse and death is associated with the novel's central symbol, the mummy, which stands for personal power handed down from native rulers in pre-Conquest times to present-day dictators. Concretely, it symbolizes the dictator himself, who, like it, has ended as a relic of the past in Paris. Equally, since it is partly a fake and had been given to France for propaganda purposes, it also symbolizes the "method," the dictator's repertoire of deceits and expedients.

Within the fairly symmetrical shape of the novel, based on the rising and falling fortunes of the dictator, the technique as we have seen, is one of alternation between the man himself and the public figure as well as between Europe and America, with each of these dualities commenting ironically on the other. A similar alternation is visible in the shifting narrative voice and the rotation of tenses. Carpentier is able to deflect the narrative viewpoint at will from that of the dictator himself to an outside observer. The latter is sometimes distanced but also sometimes ready to narrate in the first-person plural, as if enjoying a conspiratorial collusion with the central figure. This gives great flexibility, making satirical commentary easy and juxtaposing one narrator with another to point a contrast or underline an irony. First-person narration is, however, used sparingly after the opening and generally conveys something serious. Significantly it is used once for the dictator's daughter when she suddenly rediscovers her Latin American identity on tasting a piece of maize bread. The coexistence of different tenses in unexpected proximity to each other subtly implies that the dictator is unwilling or unable to differentiate clearly among past, present, and future. It suggests that he is cut off from a true vision of temporal progress. A number of indications show that the whole narrative is retrospective, and even the present-tense passages refer to the past in which the dictator is trapped. Whereas in *La consagración de la primavera* the past and the present of the characters interact in a sense dialectically to produce a new future, here the tenses are merely shuffled because only the Student, one supposes, can foresee the "true"—revolutionary—future.

While García Márquez tries in *El otoño del patriarca* to destroy the myth of executive power by exaggerating it to incredible proportions, Carpentier attacks it by making his dictator a man of limited intelligence, living precariously on his political wits. In this way the reader is forced to reflect on why such a figure can achieve and retain control over the state. The function of the humor (which critics have tended to ignore) is to maintain a delicate balance in the reader between sympathy, of a sort, with the dictator as a droll individual, and self-distancing from him as the man responsible for a regime supported by corruption and oppression. But the seriocomic approach also raises questions about the political context that allows such a dictator to operate: the complicities he relies on and the political immaturity of his fellow citizens. To this extent, and to the extent that it consistently stimulates thought rather than mere indignation, *El recurso del método* takes its place alongside García Márquez's novel and Roa Bastos's *Yo el Supremo* to form a memorable trio of portraits of dictators.

Chapter Eight
Last Works

Carpentier's Evolving Fictional Theory

Carpentier's ideas about the novel have not produced much critical comment. As is all too usual, his ideas in general, especially about time and about "'the marvelous real," have been much discussed; his practice as a novelist, that is to say, his fictional technique, has attracted some attention, though less than it deserves; but his theory of fiction is generally mentioned only in passing. It can only be dealt with summarily here, basing the discussion primarily on "De lo real maravillosamente americano" (Concerning marvelous American reality, 1964), which incorporated the 1949 preface to *El reino de este mundo;* "Problemática de la actual novela latinoamericana" (Problems of the present-day Latin American novel, 1964); "Papel social del novelista" (The social role of the novelist, 1967); "Problemática del tiempo y el idioma en la moderna novela latinoamericana" (Problems of time and language in the modern Latin American novel, 1975); and "La novela latinoamericana en vísperas de un nuevo siglo" (The Latin American novel on the eve of a new century, 1979). All of these are relatively late essays and reflect chiefly the last stage of Carpentier's outlook.

We must begin from the idea that creative writing is in some sense cognitive. It produces or contains knowledge of a different order from that which comes from scientific or rational investigation, insights perhaps akin to those perceived by the eye of faith, but which are to many writers and some critics just as valid. This, quite as much as the discovery and description of the marvelousness of Latin American reality, is the kernel of Carpentier's most famous essay, the first of those listed above. It is "the truths of the imagination" that Carpentier emphasizes here when he speaks "of a privileged revelation of reality, of an unusual or singularly favoured illumination of the unnoticed riches of reality, of an amplification of the scales and categories of reality, perceived with a particular intensity by virtue of an exaltation of the spirit which carries it to a kind of outer limit."[1] It is the faith that the writer has in this gift of special awareness that seems to have made Carpentier, in Haiti, understand that the same quality of "faith" that allowed the slaves to believe in Mackandal's magic powers also allowed the creative writer to believe in his ability to recognize other dimensions of reality especially perceptible in Latin America.

This idea of a sort of cognitive insight is referred to again and developed in "Problemática de la actual novela latinoamericana" when Carpentier once more insists on the duty of the novelist to try to reach what he calls "the deepest level—the really transcendental aspect—of things,"[2] for this is its universal aspect. What is new in this essay is Carpentier's stress on the fact that observation, in the conventional documentalist sense, is unable to produce this level of insight. On two occasions near the beginning of this essay, he underlines the dual imperative that operates on the genuinely creative novelist. One requirement is, as we have just seen, to get behind "tipicismos y costumbrismos," that is, behind what is merely characteristic and picturesque, using methods of investigation and exploration that go beyond mere narration. By such means, Carpentier affirms, it is possible to break the existing molds of fiction and produce something new and different. Just as earlier, in referring to the marvelousness of Latin American reality, he had postulated both the discovery of new levels of reality and a new mode of cognition to explore them with, so here he once more uses the same word, "revelation." But this time he goes on to suggest, as the second imperative, the need to explore Latin America's cities as a whole new area of discovery. At the same time he mentions more patient observation, backed up by deeper cultural awareness, as essential to the exploratory process. How deep this cultural awareness needs to be in order to fertilize the "deep truth, which is that of the author himself," is explained by the doctrine of "contexts," which fills out the essay. "Contexts" are the conditioning factors that operate on the reality observable to the novelist, factors he must take continuously into account if he is to understand that reality in depth.

In the course of his discussion, under the heading "Ideological Contexts," Carpentier deals with the risky question of committed literature, which he had tended to brush aside in passing in the 1949 preface to *El reino de este mundo.* Now, in Castro's Cuba, his approach is more cautious. Moreover, the reference to the Cuban

Revolution and the Bay of Pigs incident suggests that *La consagración de la primavera* was already in his mind. At this point Carpentier's views are singular and somewhat illogical. Novels of committed social comment and denunciation, he urges, should be written only after the event. That is, they should base themselves on happenings that have already taken place, rather than seek to raise the level of the reader's politicosocial awareness by means of stories about imaginary events. We recognize here, perhaps, an implicit attempt at self-justification on Carpentier's part for not having himself written the other kind of committed novels (i.e., the more imaginary kind), which Cuban literary pundits in the Castro period have predictably come to advocate.

What really characterizes "Problemática de la actual novela latinoamericana," however, is Carpentier's introduction of a fresh concept: that of the "epic" novel. This will not be based, for example, on psychological analysis, which Carpentier regards as a played-out European preoccupation, but on the conflicts between collective groups within given communities (social classes, for example; sectors, such as the military; or minorities such as Indians or mulattoes). That is to say, Carpentier's initial theory, which led him to return more than once to the idea that the writer must "name" aspects of the real in Latin America, was based on causing things that had been unperceived before to be seen and recognized. Until writers wrote about them, certain features of Latin American life and reality had remained invisible. Such features were perhaps chiefly present in the past of rural Latin America. Later Carpentier recognized the importance of urban settings. But now it is something quite different: the conflictive pattern of contemporary Latin American society is the epic novelist's field of observation. The difficulty, as Carpentier recognizes, is to discover adequately representative individuals to embody concretely the conflicts in question. This is an important consideration in the evaluation of *La consagración de la primavera,* his own "epic" novel in this sense.

Practically everything that Carpentier wrote about the novel after the two basic essays of *Tientas y diferencias* we have just mentioned was in one way or another a restatement or a development of the views they contain. Thus the idea of the "epic" novel reappears without significant change of approach in "Uncamino de medio siglo" and "Problemática del tiempo y el idioma en la moderna novela latinoamericana," both included in *Razón de ser.*[3] The concept of the baroque as the style most suited to Latin American art, including writing, which emerged near the end of "Problemática de la actual novela latinoamericana" is greatly developed and related to the idea of "the marvelous real" in "Lo barroco y lo real maravilloso." Whether or not we find convincing Carpentier's theory of the baroque (largely adapted from the ideas of the Spanish writer Eugenio D'Ors) as the expression throughout history of an art of cultural symbiosis, it tells us little more than we knew in 1964: that Latin American novelists need not fear it. Unlike the idea of "epic" fiction, it does not tell us what a modern baroque novel should actually be like, except insofar as Carpentier advocates the incorporation of all types of Latin American vocabulary into the style. For more details we need to turn to "La novela latinoamericana es vísperas de un nuevo siglo." Here Carpentier clarifies his late outlook to the extent of proclaiming the need to cut loose not only from the European tradition of the psychological novel but also from the aseptic detachment of the "objective" novel, accepting, along with *barroquismo,* melodrama, black and white characterization, and political commitment. We can easily see that this is a regressive stance, looking backward to features of the Latin American novel of the past, with its history of artistic inadequacy.

What is perhaps not present already in the *Tientas y diferencias* essays is the sense of a conflict between the writer's literary culture and the growing technification of life in our time. The background to this is Carpentier's continuing obsession with the Latin American writer's need to create the reality to which he is referring. When a European writer mentions an oak, his readers normally possess a mental picture of the kind of tree in question. But when a Latin American writer mentions a *ceiba* or an *ombú,* many of his readers may have no idea at all what such trees look like. But this is only one aspect of the question. More intractable is the problem of how a writer without specialist training can bring into being for us the marvelousness of the technology that nowadays dominates our lives when he himself cannot understand it or when it is important to the state, for instance, to keep it secret. The last stage of Carpentier's writings on the novel is full of an unresolved doubt as to whether the idea of a (baroque) "epic" novel such as he advocates will in fact be possible or meaningful in a technological society from whose workings the writer, as such, is increasingly excluded. Nonetheless the notion that the creative mind has access to a privileged area of

knowledge remains. It is restated once more, forcibly, in "Papel
social del novelista," where Carpentier argues confidently that even
without specific technological training writers can still be seen "ex-
ercising a kind of shamanism, that is, a putting into audible language of a message that at the beginning can be vacillating, formless,
hardly enunciated, and that reaches the interpreter, the mediator,
in fits and starts, in irregular breaths. There never was a better term
for it: to receive the movements of humanity, to take note of their
presence, to define and describe their collective activity."[4]

   Reasons why Carpentier's essays on fiction have remained somewhat neglected are not hard to find. On close reading the arguments
can be seen to ramble, wandering usually into reminiscences, so
that the residue, in terms of serious affirmations, is not large. For
our purposes, what matters is, after the emphasis on the need for
real technical proficiency, which we find in the early journalism,
Carpentier's insistence on the role of the novelist as mediator between
the reader and hidden dimensions of reality. As time went on this
came to be more and more associated with the hidden reality of
collective movements in history, a theme that links *El reino de este
mundo* at one end of Carpentier's production with *La consagración de
la primavera* at the other. But such a role for the author involves
him in implicitly rejecting a major element in the best Latin American fiction of our time. That is, its questioning of the real, its
insistence on the ambiguity and even the incomprehensibility in
the last analysis both of the world inside ourselves and the world
outside. That sense of mystery is present in "Viaje a la semilla."
But Carpentier seems progressively to have eliminated it from his
late work and leaves no room for it in his theory.

Concierto barroco

   The origins of Carpentier's interest in Vivaldi and his opera composed in 1733 on the theme of the Mexican emperor Montezuma
are explained in his 1975 lecture in Caracas, "Afirmación literaria
americanista." As far back as 1937 the Italian composer Malipiero
had drawn his attention to the possible existence of the work and
he had made some fruitless enquiries. It was not until the early
1970s that a French musicologist, Roland de Candé, revived his
interest in it. Carpentier discovered the lost libretto and in the
course of his investigations was able to document a meeting among

Vivaldi, Scarlatti, and Handel in Venice during the Christmas carnival of 1709. This meeting inspired the novella. It carries the dateline "Havana-Paris 1974." It was published in November of that year and since Carpentier had found Giusti's libretto in 1972 we can reasonably assume that it was written somewhere between those two dates. Carpentier was still writing *El recurso del método* in 1973; hence it is likely that the composition of the two books overlapped, given the author's habit of preparing more than one work at a time. In the end only some five months separated the publication of the two books.

Although Carpentier referred to the novella as "a kind of verbal fiesta,"[5] it would be a mistake to regard it as a mere pastiche designed for erudite entertainment. The episode in which Ofelia changes the pictures in the dictator's Parisian flat in *El recurso del método* illustrates how Carpentier liked to interrelate artistic and political change. This interrelation is postulated again in *Concierto barroco* and dominates its whole arrangement, an additional feature of which, noted by Renaud Richard,[6] is that the novella's eight chapters seem to follow the three-movement (quick-slow-quick) pattern of the classical concerto. The principal event of the story is the staging in Venice by Vivaldi of his opera *Motezuma* (sic) allegedly as a result of meeting the unnamed Mexican traveler who is the central character. But, as always, we must distinguish between story and theme. The story here concerns the Mexican's visit to Europe, theoretically in 1709, his reactions to Spain and Venice, his amusements, the meeting with Handel, Scarlatti, and Vivaldi, the staging of the opera, and the Mexican's return home. But the theme, as Jansen suggests,[7] is the effect of cultural contact between the New World and the Old.

If Carpentier had merely been interested in fictionalizing his discovery of the 1709 meeting of the three musicians and the staging of the first European opera with a Latin American theme, it would have been enough to have introduced the wealthy Mexican alone. But there are his two servants. We notice that the first, who dies, is an Indian, while the second, Filomeno, is a black. The replacement of the former by the latter is a clear reference to the dying off of the American Indians and the importation of black slaves. The white master and his Indian and black servants taken together, that is, symbolize American man, just as the three composers who meet in Venice symbolize European culture, especially musical culture. Once we recognize this, the story becomes much more than an amusing anecdote.

It is in fact a semiallegory of cultural cross-fertilization, the important point for Carpentier being the fact that it is the minor, the peripheral culture, that influences the major one. Once more the beginning of the work is characterized by typical Carpentier foreshadowing techniques. The first paragraph, with its repetition of the word "silver," stresses the wealth of the Mexican, soon to be contrasted with the poverty and squalor of Europe. But since the meaning of the story is cultural, the significance is that, without the "wealth" supplied by America, European culture would be poor indeed, as Vivaldi himself points out, suiting the action to the words by writing his opera. Its theme, the fall of the Aztec monarchy, is foreshadowed by a picture by a European painter hanging on the wall of the Mexican's drawing room in Coyacán.

Later Filomeno beats out jazz rhythms during the concert that Vivaldi and the others improvise in the novella's central scene. He finally becomes Monsieur Philomène, a jazz trumpeter in Paris and admirer of Louis Armstrong. Such fertilization of the European musical tradition by popular jazz from America, using Afro-Cuban rhythms familiar to Spanish Americans from the Caribbean, is in its turn foreshadowed by the description of the music that celebrated the defeat of the pirate Girón in chapter 2, played by whites from Europe and America, half-castes, Naborí indians, and blacks. Nor should we overlook the mixture of Mexican *mañanitas* and Italian airs that Francisquillo plays for his master in chapter 1. In the concert in chapter 5 all the baroqueness (in the sense of a harmonic and novel confluence of different cultural currents, out of which fresh patterns of creativity will emerge) reaches a delirious climax. The diverse musical traditions of northern and southern Europe combine with Filomeno's Afro-American rhythms in a synthesis that is not only full of promise of cultural renewal but is also intended to portend (revolutionary) social renewal. We notice that Filomeno's master does not take part in the musicmaking. This is because one of his roles is to revitalize European culture, not by providing new musical techniques, as Filomeno does, but by suggesting new (American) themes. Thus the contributions of master and servant complement each other. But the Mexican aristocrat does lead the symbolic dance. Second, as the jam-session concert comes to an end, Filomeno catches sight of a picture of Eve tempted by the serpent:

an allegory of birth brought about by breaking the rules. In this case it refers to the eventual birth of a new musical tradition. The chanting of "Kabala-sum-sum-sum" reminds us that the whole novella (and this central incident especially) is intended to illustrate a hidden pattern of change, in which musical cross-fertilization symbolizes historical progress (in Carpentier's view, toward the triumph of Marxist ideas).

The descriptions of the picnic and of Vivaldi's *Motezuma,* which follow, underline the fact that this hidden pattern is at first concerned with cultural change. This is the theme of the conversation during the picnic, in which the first glaring anachronisms are introduced. The composers discover the tomb of Stravinsky (buried in 1971) and discuss his work. As they leave the picnic they witness the funeral of Richard Wagner (which took place in Venice in 1883). Both Stravinsky and Wagner radically renewed the musical idiom of their times. They did so, Carpentier is implying, by using the same syncretic approach that he is advocating here, harmonizing apparently disparate elements from past and present, from classical and popular traditions, and from different geographical origins in the sort of "baroque" way symbolized by the concert in the Ospedale and the concluding Louis Armstrong concert.

But *Concierto barroco* does not contain only an allegory of musical or cultural cross-fertilization. For, as we see more fully worked out in *La consagración de la primavera,* where Stravinsky's *Rite of Spring* is used to symbolize political renewal as well, Carpentier sees cultural and political change taking place hand in hand. Here we may return to the complementarity of the Mexican traveler and his servant. They arrived in Venice in 1709, during which year the concert and the picnic take place. But as we have seen, the picnic "contains" the years 1883 and 1971. This encapsulation of the future in the present relates to the way in which the present of culture contains its past traditions, the way in which the past includes, in a sense, the future, symbolized by the presence of Handel in Stravinsky's work. But between chapters 6 and 7—that is, between the end of the picnic and the performance of *Motezuma*—in one night of sleep we leap forward from 1709 to 1733. This contrasts brusquely with the time-encapsulation earlier. It brings us back to historical change and to the Mexican, who is a wealthy *criollo,* a native-born Latin American. The performance of the opera revives in him his dormant nationalistic feelings. First this is because it becomes clear to him

that Vivaldi's appropriation of the American theme, which he ar-
rogantly uses as the basis for an essentially European work, distorts
and stylizes it and includes a strong element of cultural imperialism.
In turn this provokes in the Mexican a crisis of political conscience
so that he sees himself as having betrayed his responsibilities out
of sloth and folly. He discovers, that is, his "task," his role as an
actor on the stage of history, and returns to Mexico implicitly to
join those of his class who were preparing the ground for the struggle
for independence from Spain.

Filomeno, the man of the masses, stays behind. His time is not
yet come. For him to find his place in Latin America, he reflects,
a revolution would be needed (implicitly that led by Castro in Cuba).
For him the future is as yet only in his music. As Louis Armstrong
plays music that links the Bible and Handel to electric guitars and
Cuban drums under a ceiling decorated by Tiepolo, America at last
triumphs. What began when *criollos,* Afro-Americans, American
Indians, and Europeans made music together to celebrate Golomón's
victory in the seventeenth century now ends with Armstrong playing
music with American rhythms "like an arrow toward the future"[8]
in a Venetian palace. For Carpentier, jazz as a musical phenomenon
is always associated with the revolution. Filomeno portends Gaspar
Blanco in *La consagración de la primavera.* His trumpet at the end of
Concierto barroco is similarly associated with "the moment of settling
accounts with swine and sons of bitches" (79), that is, with the
advent of the revolution.

Plainly, then, *Concierto barroco* is more than the light-hearted
verbal fiesta its author suggested it was. It contains some of the
most prominent motifs of his later work and constitutes a prologue
to *La consagración de la primavera.*

La consagración de la primavera

In October 1975 Carpentier told an interviewer that he was more
than halfway through writing a new novel, *La consagración de la
primavera.*[9] Two years later, in December 1977, he mentioned to
another that it was finished.[10] Given that by the 1970s his rhythm
of production had long been set, we can presume that he must have
begun writing it soon after finishing *El recurso del método* and *Concierto
barroco.* As was the case with *El siglo de las luces* and *El recurso del
método* as well as *El reino de este mundo* in which he incorporated,

almost as they stood, passages from his abandoned novel *El clan disperso*, so here he incorporated into chapter 34 a long section from another abandoned novel, called, in 1964, *El año 59*, and in 1972 *Los convidados de plata*. It is the section in which Enrique returns from Caracas to Cuba and reflects on his experiences in the Venezuelan capital. Judging from the other chapters published with it in 1972, the hero of this novel was to have been one of Castro's guerrilla fighters. Evidently Carpentier later gave up this idea, perhaps because he had no direct experience of the fighting on which to base it.

The questions raised by *La consagración de la primavera* are not exclusively literary ones. As we have seen, Carpentier was always a man of left-wing sympathies, a friend and admirer of the Mexican revolutionary painter Diego Rivera, an opponent of Machado in Cuba, a supporter of the Spanish Republic and much later of the Venezuelan Communist party. But until his final return to Cuba, his position after the 1930s was cautious and even ambiguous. His writings had frequently highlighted the betrayals, difficulties, and setbacks that accompany revolutionary activity and lead to disenchantment and cynicism. Now, in his last major fictional work, this man who in the Spanish Civil War had avoided personal engagement in the struggle, who had left Cuba a second time for a comfortable and remunerative post in reactionary Venezuela, and who had waited for Castro to triumph before returning to Havana, where his prestige would ensure him an official position, was seen vicariously taking part in the fight against fascism in Spain and then in the battle of the Bay of Pigs. This man who had stood aside, living the life of art, rewriting the scene of Sofía's break with Hugues in *El siglo de las luces* fifteen times to get it right, was now, with implicit *mea culpas*, for the first time openly preaching heroic sacrifice and commitment to the Communist cause.

Those to the far left of the Communist party who had noted his attacks on direct action and his defense of gradualness in *El acoso* and *El recurso del método* recognized afresh the orthodox party-liner. Those in the party itself, with its long tradition of suspicion of unreliable writers and intellectuals, especially those of bourgeois origin, recognized the latecomer to the feast, the opportunist finally dropping the mask of bourgeois conformity now that it was safe to do so. Those opposed to Castro and Communism recognized a traitor to the ideal of the uncommitted intellectual, the conscious artist

who is dedicated to analysis and criticism from a position outside
crude class or political allegiances. Worse still, reading the novel
in conjunction with some of Carpentier's latter, more strongly worded
defenses of himself as a Marxist writer, his disingenuous attempts
to reinterpret aspects of *Ecue-Yamba-O* and *El siglo de las luces* along
appropriately left-wing lines, together with his praise of Castro and
his exaltation of the historical importance of the Bay of Pigs, opponents of his outlook saw in the ending of the novel groveling
adulation of a regime characterized by some of the very features of
fanaticism, cruelty, and betrayal of ideals that he himself had previously castigated.

Not surprisingly, then, early criticism of *La consagración de la
primavera* contained very mixed reactions, including a certain dis-
missiveness. The novel is self-evidently conceived in terms of old-
style committed writing, avoiding obtrusive technical innovations
and with a clear and unequivocal "message" rammed home relentlessly from end to end of the text. After having poked delightful
fun in *El recurso del método* at a right-wing dictator who insisted on
seeing the political struggle in black and white terms of "our fellows"
and "the cuckolds and sons of bitches" who were the enemy, Carpentier now comes uncomfortably close to adopting the same position himself the other way around.

It seems as though the intensification of Carpentier's allegiance
to revolutionary socialism after his return to Cuba produced a literary
conversion as well. "I wasn't very interested nowadays in the makers
of literature," Enrique, the hero of *La consagración de la primavera*
remarks. "A cleft had been made in my own history, separating my
present self from the aesthete-self which had gone to Europe, one
day, in search of truths—transcendental truths—which had finally
faded away before my eyes like deceitful mirages . . . Valéry,
Ortega, Breton . . . what the hell did they matter to me, if they
had never answered satisfactorily the questions that had most an-
guished me."[11]

The novel is basically the story of Vera, an émigré Russian ballet-
dancer who has fled from the Russian Revolution, and Enrique, the
son of wealthy Cuban parents, who has gone over to the left. Its
theme is spelled out by Vera on the penultimate page: "I, a bourgeois
with bourgeois parents and grandparents, had fled as fast as I could
from anything like revolution, only to end by living in the bosom
of a revolution . . . Enrique, a bourgeois with bourgeois parents

and grandparents, had fled from his bourgeois world in search of something different which in the end turned out to be the Revolution which had now brought us together again" (575). After participating in the Spanish Civil War, where he meets Vera, Enrique lives with her in France until the approach of World War II sends them back to Cuba. There he becomes an architect, but through involvement with anti-Batista activities, he is forced to flee to Venezuela until the triumph of Castro. Vera teaches ballet, but as she is about to mount a performance of Stravinsky's *Rite of Spring* in Paris, her school is shot up by Batista's police as a center of subversion. She escapes to live quietly at the other end of the island. With the triumph of the Revolution Enrique and Vera separately accept the new regime, but only Enrique's participation in the Bay of Pigs fighting, where he is wounded, produces a full reconciliation between them.

The novel is a reworking of the theme of enthusiasm-disenchantment with regard to revolutionary endeavor, which underlies *El siglo de las luces*. Much of Carpentier's work tends toward the contrapuntal, the dualistic. Notably in *El siglo de las luces, El recurso del método*, and *La consagración de la primavera*, this dualism is visible in the pendular swing of the setting from Europe to America and back. It is present also in the characterization: Esteban vis-à-vis Sofía, the Dictator vis-à-vis the Student, and here Enrique vis-à-vis Vera. But there is a special difference in this case. Vera's activities in relation to ballet include a kind of commentary on Enrique's ideological development, which is the basic subject of the novel. For this reason her discovery of Calixto and other black dancers from the poor suburbs of Havana, a discovery that lifts her out of routine and disappointment with her work, through rediscovery of the popular, communal art of dance, coincides with the central turning point of the work. Equally it explains the choice of the title. Stravinsky's *Rite of Spring*, it is suggested, had been seen up to that point as a magnificent failure, its theme centered on sacrifice. Suddenly Vera sees it as a potential success, an affirmation, its theme now centering not on the sacrifice but on the ensuing fecundity.

The passage, in chapter 16, is of crucial importance not only for this novel. Hitherto all of Carpentier's work had tended to emphasize sacrifice and enthusiasm in vain. Now the Cuban Revolution had reoriented his outlook. The sacrifice, the waste, the disillusionment are still there, represented by the loss of the Spanish Civil War at the beginning of the book. But they are now no longer in vain, as Gaspar Blanco, the black revolutionary musician, is there to prophesy: "time in the end always justifies those who have shown themselves faithful to certain principles" (254). For now it is offset by the success of the Cuban Revolution. The Dance of Death is turned into a Dance of Life by the intervention of the "real" people, in this case the blacks, with their untaught artistry. Not for nothing does *The Rite of Spring* become the "objective" of Vera's life. It symbolizes revolution and the rediscovery of meaningfulness, just after she hears of Fidel Castro for the first time.

The choice of Vera as a partner for Enrique is dictated by Carpentier's will to establish a connection between the Cuban Revolution and the Russian Revolution. The meeting of the couple during the Spanish Civil War is similarly part of an attempt to situate the latter as an unsuccessful interlude between two major historical events: the first triumph of Communism in Europe and its first triumph in Latin America. As Jansen points out,[12] the relationship between Enrique and Vera as well as their respective evolutions are intended to illustrate the dialectical process by which, according to Marxist ideas, historical progress comes about. Enrique begins life in the novel as a dilettante revolutionary, "a rich guy with a sense of shame, balls, and some sort of social conscience" (255), as Gaspar, the representative of Marxist orthodoxy, defines him. The first phase of his evolution begins when he is forced to flee to Europe after a childish attempt to assassinate the dictator Gerardo Machado. In Paris he meets a German-Jewish girl, Ada. Her fate at the hands of the Nazis produces in him an increased political awareness, which takes him into one of the International Brigades fighting for the Republic of Spain. But after his return to Cuba he begins to wonder if this early participation in the class struggle had not been merely a prolongation of his adolescence. The years of World War II are years of transition and conformity for him, marked by his affair with his rich bourgeois cousin, Teresa. Only with the growth of repression in Cuba does his rebelliousness surface again as he assists the anti-Batista urban guerrillas. The comment of his more corrupted friend José Antonio—"At the right time Enrique showed us that not everything in him was lost" (419)— is a clear signal from Carpentier to the reader that a third phase of Enrique's evolution is in gestation. Predictably the shift comes when he hears a speech by Fidel Castro in Caracas. It motivates his decision to return to Cuba and join the Revolution. The culmination of this final phase is Enrique's participation in the fighting at the Bay of Pigs, where he makes the blood-sacrifice for the new Cuba, which, linked to his wound in the Spanish Civil War, consecrates him as a genuine freedom fighter.

Vera's evolution is different from Enrique's. He is always potentially a revolutionary. She, on the other hand, has been deeply traumatized by the Russian Revolution of 1917. Thereafter she is a passive figure, at the mercy of events, which carry her from Baku to Petrograd, London, and Paris, and thence to Santiago de Cuba and finally to Baracoa. Up to the end of chapter 29 she is consciously apolitical, hating the idea of revolution, seeking refuge in dance, and, as we see in chapter 1, seeing reality through literary spectacles. Only contact with her friend Olga, the wife of a French collaborator with the Nazis, provokes her to accept vaguely left-wing principles. Her true ideal is art, as José Antonio, who has betrayed it, recognizes. But the ideal is shattered by the wanton destruction of her ballet company. At the same time she realizes that Enrique has been Teresa's lover, off and on, for fifteen years. Her whole fragile world collapses during her crisis at the end of chapter 33. While Enrique's evolution has ups and downs, Vera's is more consistent. She cultivates the dual illusion that art as a public activity and love as private fulfillment will be enough to give life meaning. When both collapse together the way is left clear for Carpentier to point her toward the growing realization that such bourgeois, individualistic ideals have to be underpinned by a collective politicosocial faith. This Vera gradually accepts in Baracoa.

Both Enrique's and Vera's characters are ideological at bottom. Harking back to the confidence of the slaves in Santo Domingo, to Esteban's reflections before the Crucifix, and to the Student's thoughts in Notre Dame, Carpentier is once more asserting the need for life-supporting beliefs. At the end of chapter 15 Vera had recognized: "I have no faith in anything." After her crisis, she perceives that she is again "without the necessary compass of faith in something" and that similarly Enrique has lost all faith in architecture (432). In contrast Gaspar produces envy in Enrique by his "solid faith" in Marxism. The climax of the book brings the achievement of this faith and of willingness to sacrifice for it on the parts of both Vera and Enrique. In this they join the rest of the Cuban people, who are said to have formerly had no faith in anything, but after the

revolution find faith again. We notice, however, that neither Enrique nor Vera attains genuine attachment to the revolution by direct
study and absorption of revolutionary doctrine, though Enrique does
read Marx. Art and creativity are mediating forces in both cases.
Enrique begins to evolve politically when he begins to appreciate
modern art. Vera's shift occurs unconsciously at first, when she
reinterprets the meaning of *The Rite of Spring*. But Carpentier is
careful to suggest that only when art is linked to an ideal of social
progress does it really reinforce Marxism's gift of existential
confidence.

Angel Rama's[13] comment that with the exception of a few secondary figures, such as Teresa, the characterization in *La consagración
de la primavera* is unconvincing, seems unduly harsh. To be sure,
the respective evolutions of Enrique and Vera are carefully stage
managed, just as are those of Esteban and Sofía in *El siglo de las
luces*. We feel an uneasy awareness at intervals that they are being
instrumentalized a little too obviously to develop the theme. But
on first reading the novel this sensation is only sporadic. What tends
to provoke more protest in the reader is the overrigid framework
created around them by the other characters. Carpentier's intention
is to provide us with a fully graduated table of bourgeois and an-
tibourgeois attitudes against which we can read off, as it were, the
relative positions of the central couple. At one end of the scale we
have Enrique's aunt, the Countess, who epitomizes the arrogant
selfishness, philistinism, and resistance to change of a grotesquely
overprivileged class. Teresa, his cousin, is a degree nearer accept-
ability, because of her apparent refusal to conform to her mother's
pseudovalues. But we are carefully warned in chapter 32 that she
is a Fascist at heart. José Antonio, the artist turned advertising
consultant, is closer still to enjoying the reader's sympathy, but is
shown in the end to be a mere time-server. He is on the right side,
however, in contrast to Hans "el catire" of chapters 8 and 9, who,
like a mirror-image of José Antonio, subsequently emerges as a radio
announcer for Nazi Germany.

In contrast to this group of reactionaries stand Gaspar and Calixto,
both blacks, both Communists, both totally committed. Not for
nothing is Gaspar's faith in communism in the forefront of Vera's
mind when her world collapses in chapter 33, while Calixto is among
Fidel Castro's triumphant troops when they arrive in Havana in
1959. In between Gaspar and Calixto stands Mirta, Vera's pupil,

gradually overcoming her racial and class prejudices just as Enrique and Vera do. At the wider level we see the same duality at work in the repeated descriptions of pre-Castro Cuban society as corrupt, racist, gringoistic, and philistine, while the triumphant Castro troops are naively presented as belonging to a new category of mankind. The arrangement of it all has a tidiness that is unreal. Ideology has overtaken art. For all that, the objection to *La consagración de la primavera* at this level is not that it is ideologically motivated, for so, willy-nilly, is all literature. The objection is that the ideology is oversimple and too near the surface. The danger is that instead of stimulating the reader, the mere act of reading this sort of book placates him by providing in itself a surrogate for the impulse to rebel.

Of the novel's 42 chapters, slightly more than half are narrated by Vera and the rest, except for three where the narration is shared, by Enrique. In turn the chapters as a whole are grouped into nine parts with a strong tendency for the narratorial voice to remain the same throughout each part and for there to be, over all, a certain alternation. Part 1 is dominated by Enrique; part 2 by Vera; parts 3 and 4 by Enrique; parts 5, 6 and 7 by Vera (except for the interlude in Caracas, chapter 34); part 8 by Enrique; and part 9 by Enrique and then by Vera. Within this alternation we notice that the two longest parts (1 and 5) are dominated by Enrique and Vera respectively, and that, although Vera is used as a narrator more extensively after the middle of the novel, in some ways the more important sections are narrated by Enrique. These are the opening, except for the initial meeting in Spain, the central section, and the concluding section, except for the final pages. Thus Vera opens and closes the narrative, but Enrique tends to have the main impact. The distribution underscores the difference between their respective evolutions. Enrique is more committed and active, despite his phase of disenchantment after the Spanish Civil War. Vera is more passive; her evolution is slower and gathers speed only gradually even after chapter 29. Again, we must take into account that Enrique is in his own country, while Vera, as a foreigner, takes longer to adapt to the process of change in Cuba.

Although it is difficult to see it on first reading, *La consagración de la primavera* is structured rather symmetrically around chapters 21 and 22. It is at this point that we recognize the dual functionality of Gaspar Blanco. On the one hand, as we have seen, this founder-

member of the Cuban Communist party provides the standard of
conviction against which Enrique and Vera's evolutions are to be
measured. But he also has a significant role in the story. It is through
meeting him that Enrique comes to know Ada. It is through him
too that he joins an International Brigade. Above all it is through
meeting him again in Cuba in chapter 21 that Enrique is put back
on the road to revolution. Meanwhile Vera, also through Gaspar,
meets Calixto and the black dancers, who transform her notions of
ballet and of *The Rite of Spring*. Then symbolically, in chapter 22,
Stalingrad survives the attack of the German army. This is an event
that Carpentier presents as a turning point in the struggle against
Nazism comparable to the turning point Enrique and Vera have
just experienced in their private lives.

Symbolism, as always, plays an important role in *La consagración
de la primavera*. A potent example is the description of the morning
after a party for Machado in Enrique's aunt's house in chapter 3.
The wrecked decorations and the rubbish lying about represent the
death-agony of the old Cuban upper class. The technique continues
throughout the novel, from the description of New York's architecture, which symbolizes capitalism, to Enrique's loveless love-
making with Teresa, which stands for the relation of the sexes in a
bourgeois society. The central symbol is of course *The Rite of Spring*
itself, in which the sacrifice of the maiden symbolizes man's endless
sacrifices for human progress, while the final triumphant ritual dance
symbolizes the triumph of the revolution. At the same time, as we
see in chapter 32, Vera's shift of attitude toward ballet symbolizes
her own evolution toward political awareness.

At bottom there are two parallel lines of development in the
novel. One is the objective historical sequence of events; the other
is the subjective evolutions of Enrique and Vera. Her slower progress
toward political commitment is functionally set against Enrique's,
which is both earlier and eventually more complete. But in a similar
way the historical background is used to underline the direction
both of them in the end take. The keynote is revolution and counterrevolution. Four revolutionary periods are alluded to in the novel:
those of the Russian Revolution, the Mexican Revolution, the Spanish Republic, and the Cuban Revolution. Four counterrevolutionary
moments also appear: those of Nazism in the 1930s, the Franco
rebellion in Spain, collaborationism in German-occupied France in
the 1940s, and the attempted invasion of Castro's Cuba in 1961.

As is the case with the supporting cast of characters, the revolutionary references are carefully orchestrated. The Russian Revolution exists in the background to the novel. It is not presented directly and its ambiguities are at first emphasized. But Gaspar's defense of the Russo-German nonaggression pact of 1939 and the allusion to Stalingrad indicate Carpentier's favorable stance. The Mexican Revolution is briefly mentioned in chapter 5, since it was the first major "progressive" revolution in twentieth-century Latin America, in order to make two points. First, that a long time must elapse before judgment can be passed on major revolutionary events. Second, that it was only a partial revolution, since it did not relieve the crushing poverty of the masses. The Spanish experiment is used to indicate the tragic disunity of the left. The object of all this is to present the Cuban Revolution as inheriting the ideals of 1917 and avoiding the disunity and limitations of the Spanish and Mexican experiences.

Nazism, through the fate of Ana and her parents, together with the example of Hans El Catire, is the force that, even more than Machado's dictatorship in Cuba, converts Enrique from being almost politically unaware to being a soldier of the Spanish Republic. The success of the counterrevolution in Spain carries three connotations. It reminds the reader of one of Carpentier's oldest themes, the inevitability of setbacks to human endeavors for progress. Second, it emphasizes the Spenglerian idea that Europe was too corrupt for it to be possible to change society there radically. Third, that where Europe failed to follow the ideals of 1917, Latin America, led by Cuba, could succeed. The brief reference to collaborationism in France, represented by Olga's husband, is there to stress the view that the bourgeoisie will always prefer fascism to a possible left-wing alternative. Finally the attack on the Bay of Pigs is seen as the test of Cuba's revolutionary will. Uniting his own experience of defeat in Spain and victory in Cuba, Enrique symbolizes the eventual triumph of the revolution. When Vera at the very end of the novel returns to the idea of staging a new version of *The Rite of Spring,* this is what the triumph of spring, after the sacrifice, will portray.

In one of the most important statements in the novel, Carpentier is careful to remind us that the acceptance by Vera and Enrique of the advent of the revolution and their willing adjustment to it are not always historical possibilities. Thinking perhaps of Esteban and

Sofía in *El siglo de las luces,* he writes in a well-meditated affirmation: "There is an irreconcilable discrepancy between the time-scale of Man and the time-scale of History. Between the short days of a lifetime and the long, very long, years of collective happenings" (83). Understanding Vera and Enrique involves understanding what Carpentier had emphasized since *El reino de este mundo:* that private ideological evolution and individual endeavor are not always crowned with success. The end of *La consagración de la primavera* does not invalidate the end of *El siglo de las luces.*

Ultimately, however, *La consagración de la primavera* stands or falls as a work of art rather than as a contribution to the task of sensitizing people to the importance of the world class struggle. Here the critical question is posed by the novelist himself when he refers in chapter 5 to the work of the Mexican revolutionary painter Diego Rivera as "this highly figurative, narrative, furiously meaningful painting, forcing me to face the problem of its legitimacy" (64) and in the affirmation: "Revolutionary literature has no need to be a literature of outcries and insults, of proclamations and Apocalypse. One can express oneself most eloquently in a lower key" (504). Does *La consagración de la primavera* avoid the excesses of partisan writing? Does it achieve "legitimacy" as a work of art?

The answer must be: not entirely. It has in generous measure some of the great qualities of Carpentier's best writing: human insight, historical vision, superb descriptive purple passages, confident handling of the narrative voices and of the storyline. Containing as it does so much that is vaguely autobiographical, much of it rings true. But there are infelicities. Hans El Catire, for example, on whom Carpentier hangs an obtrusive sermon on political self-involvement, or Gaspar, whose faith in Marxism is distressingly uncritical, are not adequately rounded characters. The text includes self-indulgent digressions, based on the author's experiences in Paris and Caracas, which in his younger days he would probably have pruned. The presentation of New York is a caricature. The adulation of Castro is as distasteful as Victor Hugues's infatuation with Robespierre. But *La consagración de la primavera* lacks two qualities above all: ambiguity and irony. The view it presents of social reality is in the last analysis reductive; the value pattern it incorporates is over-simplified. Enrique is reported by Vera as having an ironic outlook, but the reader does not perceive it. Irony, one of Carpentier's greatest qualities as a novelist, has been sacrificed to ideology, and the sacrifice is too great. No writer of Carpentier's stature, except one determined to suppress his ironic vision, could have written the ending of *La consagración de la primavera,* which, as we have suggested elsewhere,[14] turns into a John Wayne film episode, with true grit replacing guilt and cowardice. This is not to say that the novel is not in its way memorable. But it is not Carpentier's masterpiece.

El arpa y la sombra

In 1937, while working as a producer and sound technician in France, Carpentier prepared for Radio Luxembourg a version of Paul Claudel's play about Columbus, *Le livre de Christophe Colombe.* We know, from his own statement, that just then he was steeping himself in Latin American history from Columbus on. Clearly he was to acquire some familiarity with the vast corpus of writing about the discoverer of the New World. This included both works by those who, like Claudel, exalted Columbus as a man chosen to fulfill a divinely appointed mission, and those who attempted to dispel the legends and fabrications that had grown up around the great explorer. In an interview in 1980[15] he declared that his aim in this "irreverent tale" was to express his irritation with the whole pattern of writing about Columbus that presented him as a religious visionary, a near-saint, one who as a matter of historical fact had been proposed to the Vatican as a candidate for sainthood. It is equally a matter of historical fact that the proposal came to grief partly because of evidence that Columbus had fathered a child out of wedlock. Here, then, was the probable source of Carpentier's interest in the story. But the novel, which was to be his swan song, is more than the sarcastic parody that some, especially French, critics seem to consider it. For it returns afresh to two of the obsessive motifs that since *Ecue-Yamba-O* had recurred in Carpentier's creative work: the conflict and attraction of European and Latin American cultures, and the importance of supportive myths as a factor in human effort and achievement.

In a sense *El recurso del método* had been about a myth: the myth of European cultural superiority, belied by the record of bloodshed and barbarity in the Old World and the extent to which the First World War dwarfed in scale the horrors of the dictator's campaigns. But the dictator himself, deeply aware of the power of myth to affect human outlook, attempts to convert it to his own advantage by creating a myth of origins based on the mummy. In contrast, the story of the Student showed that genuine myths grow spontaneously. The stroke suffered by the dictator while visiting the mummy symbolizes the process of false myth-creation rebounding on the creator. The truth is that what the mummy really represents is man's ageless attraction to absolute power.

In *El arpa y la sombra* the notion of deliberately fabricating a myth is worked out in greater detail and in a more epoch-making context. The novel is concerned with the attempt begun under Pope Pius IX to beatify Columbus, as a first step to proclaiming him a saint. But as it proceeds it becomes the story of a desire to create and manipulate a myth by a figure whom Carpentier regards as an aspirant to absolute spiritual power. At a wider level still, it becomes the story of yet another attempt by Europe to retard the emancipation of Latin America, this time in spiritual terms. One of Carpentier's objects in the novel, therefore, is to demythicize Columbus, to strip away the layers of pious adulation that swathe the figure of the Discoverer and to reveal the human being underneath.

In order to achieve this he was obliged to study in depth not only the writings of, and attributed to, Columbus, but also those of the creators of the Columbus myth, from Diego Columbus to Roselly de Lorgues and Leon Bloy, not forgetting Claudel, in modern times. The French critic Saint-Lu, in well-documented articles,[16] has shown that, in his desire to react against hagiographic biographies, Carpentier does not hesitate to take liberties with the evidence. Other critics have shown the extent to which Carpentier drew on material from Columbus's own writings, and in particular from Bloy, to create certain passages in the novel that can be traced point by point to these sources. Such indications are useful; but more interesting is the kind of figure Carpentier creates. It is that of a picaresque individual, a not unattractive rogue, role-playing, debauched, unscrupulous, quick-witted, ambitious for rank, and yet insecure, resentful, and constantly at odds with himself. An ambiguous figure, partly sincere, partly hypocritical, boastful but self-aware, cynical yet, on his deathbed, ready for a—carefully graduated—degree of penitence.

The longest of the novel's three parts, the central one, is wholly devoted to Columbus the man. It takes the form of a long, monologue flashback, supposedly running through his mind as he prepares for his last confession. Its function is to fit the historical data into the interpretation of Columbus as someone quite the opposite of a saint. The details of his origins and early life, his travels, his growing belief in a western route across the Atlantic, and his tribulations before setting out, as well as his voyages and returns, are generally taken from well-known sources. What matters is the principle of selection Carpentier applies to them and the imaginary details he adds. The criterion he employs is that of consistently contradicting the Columbus "legend," whether it originated with the Discoverer himself or with later biographers.

With gentle irony Carpentier begins his portrait of the potential saint by presenting him as a lecher. He continues it with a description of him as a liar, a charlatan, and a hypocrite, to say nothing of being a renegade Jew with few religious scruples. He brings it to a climax by presenting the voyage of 1492 as a commercial speculation begun by trickery and finally arranged between Queen Isabella of Castile and Columbus while they are in bed together. On his arrival in the New World, Columbus specifically disowns any intention of putting propagation of the Faith first. On the contrary, he is terrified of finding Christianity already there. His aim is to glorify himself by stealing a march on the Church, taking Christianity to the Indies by the western route before it can reach them from the East. Finally, unable to find gold, which is his secondary obsession—his primary one is his own pride and ambition—he institutes slavery in the New World, despite deciding that it was the original site of the Garden of Eden. Doubly forsworn, since he failed to keep two vows to the Virgin; a swindler, since he knew from the outset that there were lands west of Iceland; invoking the Christian aspect of the Discovery only when gold and slaves had failed to fulfill his purpose, he is seen at length rather as an emissary of the Devil than as Christo-phoros. What prevents him from degenerating into a mere scoundrel is the humor that surrounds his account of his life. Its first function is, as in *El recurso del método*, to preserve our sympathy for Columbus while allowing Carpentier to get on with demythicizing him. Later, again as previously, it becomes more satirical, especially in relation to the process of beatification, which is presented in a deliciously grotesque light suggesting the *esperpentos* of the Spanish writer Valle-Inclán.

Three elements of the presentation depart significantly from the mainstream of historical revisionism with regard to the Columbus legend. These are his Jewish origins; his acquaintance with Jacobo, another Jew, together with his trip to Iceland; and his sexual relations with Queen Isabella. Each is introduced to make Columbus an even less likely candidate for sainthood: his background is wrong, he did not set off into the totally unknown with pious intentions, and his enterprise was founded not merely on greed but also on lust. By adding these (probably) imaginary elements, Carpentier is creating an antimyth, using the same technique as Roselly and Bloy had used to create the original modern legend. Thus history becomes a battleground of conflicting myths, while both myth and antimyth are founded on Columbus's own self-mythification. Is Carpentier, as Leenhart suggests,[17] expressing his skepticism about the role of man in history? Hardly; the reference to Marx in the text, the presentation of the Discovery of America in strictly Marxist terms as a materialistic venture, the equally orthodox picture of Columbus as a man "alienated" by early capitalism, and the episode of a pope (who is surprisingly like Columbus in important respects) attempting to intervene in history and instrumentalize a myth so as to preserve a major element of Latin American dependency on Europe, all give pause for thought.

The story covers three phases of Latin American history: the Discovery, the independence period (when the future Pious IX visits Argentina and Chile), and the modern period, since Leo XIII died in 1903. We know that for Carpentier the three transcendental dates in Latin American history are 1492, the Discovery; 1810, the beginning of independence; and 1961, the Bay of Pigs. It is not impossible that Columbus's cryptic reference to a mysterious point on the coast of Cuba that marks the shift from one epoch to another, "which I called alpha-omega,"[18] refers to the last of these, just as Pius IX's trip to Chile contains veiled references to the Chile of the late 1970s. If this is so, we see here another example of Carpentier's vision of history as a spiral process. The myth created by Columbus serves its historical purpose of forwarding the discovery and conquest of Latin America. The countermyth of Pius IX fails. With the victory at the Bay of Pigs the interplay of myths instrumentalized by mercantilist and later by capitalist society ceases and is replaced by a dialectical and materialist interpretation of history such as the novel itself, up to a point, proposes. Carpentier may well have believed that Marxist-orientated societies themselves find uses for myths. If he did, he prudently left his audience to read between the lines.

Jacqueline Tauzin[19] has demonstrated that the structural principle governing the novel's organization is highly symmetrical, with the attempt at beatification at one end balanced by its failure at the other. The fifteen sequences of the central biographical flashback turn on the discovery of the New World and in particular of Cuba, which is thus the center of balance of the novel as a whole. The appearance of Isabella in the sixth and tenth episodes (sixth from the beginning and sixth from the end of the central section) encapsulates symmetrically the center itself. What has not so far been analyzed is Carpentier's subtle alternation of past and present verb tenses, sometimes in the same paragraph. As in *El recurso del método* the shifts, which seem arbitrary, are deliberate, now emphasizing that we are reading a flashback into which the dying Columbus occasionally intrudes, now using a historic present in order to emphasize certain events of special significance, such as Pius IX's recognition of his vocation or the moment of the Discovery. In addition the juxtaposition of different tenses is a metaphor of the inseparability of past and present.

Finally Columbus's story, as Carpentier tells it, is a parody of a journey to the Garden of Eden, yet another attempt to return to the source. Undertaken in bad faith, with materialistic motives on the one hand and for self-glorification on the other, its objective turns out to be spurious. The earthly paradise Columbus declares he has found is a mere pretence to excuse his failure to find gold. It is possible to see in *El arpa y la sombra* a meditation on the power of words and hence to see the novel as implicitly concerned with the relation between discourse and reality. In the end, however, its message is that of *Los pasos perdidos:* there is no way back to an earthly paradise (which is a fiction); there is only a way forward to new historical tasks and problems.

Chapter Nine
Conclusion

T. J. Peavler classifies Carpentier as one of the few novelists who make the full transition from the "old" novel of Spanish America to the "Boom." "Future scholars," he writes, "will undoubtedly view him as a key-figure when they place the new novel in perspective and document its history, for his works reflect not only the major waves but even the lesser ripples of the entire transitional period."[1] With the reservations advanced earlier in respect of *La consagración de la primavera* and Carpentier's late advocacy of a documentalist novel in which the novelist functions as a historian of his epoch, charting social developments, this classification of Carpentier, which would place him chronologically alongside Miguel Angel Asturias, is substantially correct in terms of literary history.

If we look at the decade of the 1930s in Spanish American fiction, we see the emergence of five major representative novelists. At one extreme J. M. Arguedas, writing about the Indians of Peru, represents the continuance of regionalism, but with a wholly new insight into the natives' mentality. At the other extreme, J. C. Onetti, in Uruguay, with *El pozo* (1939), is a totally urban novelist whose subversion of conventional attitudes toward reality, emphasis on sexuality, and incorporation of humor together with a deep existential malaise, marks what is probably the true beginning of the mainstream "new" novel. In between stand Eduardo Mallea of Argentina, Spanish America's only important psychological novelist, plowing his lone furrow, together with Asturias and Carpentier, whose joint experience of surrealism in Europe transformed their earlier regionalism into kindred forms of magical realism.

What is noticeable is that of this group only Onetti was seriously preparing to question radically and consistently the traditional view of the real. Asturias, in a famous pronouncement, recognized that the difference between the world as perceived by the conscious mind and the reality seen in dreams is "purely mechanical."[2] But like the other three novelists he was not fully prepared to query the notion of a reality outside the text against which its degree of verisimilitude could be checked. This is in many ways the basic issue. Carpentier, as we know, took an even more uncompromising stand. In retrospect we can see that his well-known comment in "Problemática del tiempo y el idioma en la moderna novela latinoamericana":

> Personally, as you know, I have tried to speculate in my own way with time. With circular time I come back to the point of departure, that is, a story that curls back on itself in *Los pasos perdidos,* and in *El Camino de Santiago.* Recurrent time, that is, inverted time, time going backwards, in *Viaje a la semilla.* The time of yesterday in today, that is to say a signified yesterday present in a signifying today in *El siglo de las luces,* in *El recurso del método,* in *Concierto barroco.* Time that circles around man without altering his essence in my story *Semejante a la noche.* . . . [3]

is more important for what it does not say than for what it says. There is no vestige of a suggestion here that the presentation of the ambiguities of time is in any sense a metaphor of the ambiguity of reality as a whole. Once we recognize this, we are able to see why Carpentier was ultimately able to make a smooth transition back to something like old-style realism in *La consagración de la primavera.*

When, therefore, Carpentier asserted in 1979 that "there is narrative autonomy, without interpretations, in authors like Julio Cortázar, Juan Rulfo, Carlos Fuentes, García Márquez, Roa Bastos and myself. It couldn't be said that there is, among us, the peculiar 'family resemblance' that one can perceive among the novelists of the previous generation,"[4] he was, in a sense, right. Significantly, however, he leaves out the one major figure with whom until 1973 he did have a "family resemblance": Vargas Llosa, whom G. M. Martin has rightly called, with regard to his work up to that date, "a critical realist."[5] There is a great deal in common between the vision of reality in Vargas Llosa's *Conversación en La Catedral* (1969) and *La consagración de la primavera.* If, that is, we accept that what characterizes the "New Novel" in Spanish America is something more than just successful experimentalism with narrative technique, an innovatory attitude to language, and the incorporation into fiction of more mythical, symbolic, and fantastic elements. If we accept the questioning and even the negation of "observed" reality as fundamental, then we must distinguish between writers whose aim is to make the reflection of "reality" seem, as it were, "more real" in the conventional sense in their work, and those whose work is designed to shake our faith in our ability to understand reality at all.

Carpentier's insistence that the "magical real" in his work is simply an extraordinary or unusual aspect of everyday reality, such as can be found frequently in Latin America (that is to say, an extension of reality, not a subversion of it) is highly relevant. In terms of Peavler's assertions, what it underlines is the transitional position of Carpentier, rather than the fullness of his transition. For in fact the only major work of his that crosses the divide completely is "Viaje a la semilla," which goes beyond the magical real into the realm of the supernatural, which is the realm of the fantastic proper. Even *El acoso, Concierto barroco,* and "Semejante a la noche," for all their technical virtuosity, are not in the same category. The last indeed illustrates the difference perfectly: in "Semejante a la noche" time changes, but reality remains substantially the same, whereas in "Viaje a la semilla" not only is time put into reverse, but reality itself is mysteriously altered, as the workmen discover.

What does this mean? The questioning of reality that we perceive in the New Novel has its roots in doubt—doubt about man's ability to recognize truth of any significant kind, to make sense of the universe, to accept the human condition as other than tragic. Such doubts go back through Borges and others to the collapse of belief we associate with the religious debate in the nineteenth century and the crisis of confidence in a fatherly world according to design that followed. Carpentier almost certainly did not harbor such doubts. If we are willing to regard as unproven his allegedly circular view of time, there is little else in his work to suggest that he found in Marxism a refuge from metaphysical despair such as was obviously the case with the Chilean poet Pablo Neruda, for example. This is no criticism of Carpentier's outlook. It is not necessarily a privilege to participate in the contemporary collapse of confidence in existence. But to recognize that Carpentier was largely unshaken by it sets him apart from writers like García Márquez, Cortázar, or Fuentes, to whom reality seems at times not just extraordinary or unusual but mysterious and uncanny, if not incomprehensible.

Arguably, however, what in the end qualifies a writer to be regarded as belonging to Spanish America's New Novelists is not so much his outlook as the international recognition his work enjoys. This is certainly Carpentier's own view in "La novela latinoamericana en vísperas de un nuevo siglo." There he contends that the test is the novelist's ability to achieve the universal without losing sight of the local. In turn this ability depends on two factors above all. The first is the acquisition of a genuinely wide and deep general culture, as distinct from the rather provincial one inside which, Carpentier tends to suggest, earlier generations of Spanish American writers were trapped. Insofar as anything can protect the novelist from being thrown onto the defensive by the technological revolution, this alone can. The other factor is one that Carpentier has tirelessly advocated since his articles from Paris in *Social* and *Carteles:* the need for conscious technical proficiency. He himself can be seen constantly updating his armory of technical skills. *El acoso* was already a tour de force. Thereafter, whether we examine the narratorial stance, use of (and techniques of avoiding) dialogue, symbolism, structural patterning, presentation of character, or modes of commentary, we find in Carpentier's work to the very end an ongoing development.

Perhaps more than anything else to be a New Novelist is to have achieved the often-mentioned *salto de calidad* (leap forward in quality), which characterizes recent fiction in Spanish America. However we interpret his evolving thought, Carpentier has consistently broken new ground thematically and come up with new solutions to the technical problems that this has involved. Despite the large number of critical articles and books devoted to it, his work, especially in its later phase, has still not been adequately assessed. But there is no question that, whatever view we take of the development of fiction in Spanish America since the 1930s, Carpentier's contribution to it will be found to be of central importance.

Notes and References

Chapter One

1. For more biographical information see Salvador Arias, ed., *Recopilación de textos sobre Alejo Carpentier* (La Habana, 1977), hereafter *Recopilación* pp. 15–70, 523–30, See also Klaus Müller-Bergh, *Alejo Carpentier: Estudio biográfico-crítico* (Long Island City, 1972), and Araceli García Carranza, "Vida y obra de Alejo Carpentier," in *Alejo Carpentier, 75° aniversario* (La Habana: Ministerio de Cultura, 1979), no page numbers. Dates and information do not always tally.

2. Margarita Fazzolari, *Paradiso y el sistema poético de Lezama Lima* (Buenos Aires: García Cambeiro, 1979), p. 71.

3. *La música en Cuba* (Mexico, 1946), p. 236, and *Recopilación*, p. 61.

4. Roberto González Echevarría, *Alejo Carpentier: The Pilgrim at Home* (Ithaca, 1977), esp. pp. 55–57.

5. Roberto González Echevarría in Joaquín Roy, ed., *Narrativa y crítica de nuestra América* (Madrid, 1978), p. 129. John S. Brushwood, "El criollismo de esencias en *Don Goyo* y *Ecue-Yamba-O*," in *Estudios de literatura hispanoamericana en honor a José J. Arrom*, ed. Andrew Debicki and Enrique Pupo-Walker, (Chapel Hill, 1974), pp. 215–25 (hereafter Arrom, *Estudios*), also insists on Carpentier's sense of the positive values of the natural condition.

6. *Ecue-Yamba-O* (Barcelona, 1979), p. 14; subsequent references are to this edition.

7. Lloyd King, *Alejo Carpentier, Caribbean Writer* (St. Augustine, 1977), p. 9.

8. Joseph Sommers, "Ecue-Yamba-O: semillas del arte narrativo de Alejo Carpentier," in Arrom, *Estudios*, pp. 227–38.

9. Esther Mocega-González, *Alejo Carpentier: estudios sobre su narrativa* (Madrid, 1980), p. 146.

10. "Un gesto de peligrosa afirmación animal," in *Ecue-Yamba-O*, the Buenos Aires, Xanadú, 1968 edition. The last word has been prudently dropped from the 1979 edition.

11. Pedro M. Barreda-Tomás, "Alejo Carpentier: dos visiones del negro, dos conceptos de la novela," *Hispania* 55 (1972):35.

12. "La época, las tendencias . . . nos imponían sus deformaciones, su ecología verbal, sus locas proliferaciones de metáforas, de símiles mecánicos, su lenguaje puesto al ritmo de la estética futurista (porque, lo vemos ahora, todo salió de allí . . .) que al fin y al cabo, estaba engen-

drando una nueva retórica." *Ecue-Yamba-O, prólogo* to the 1979 edition, p. 7.

13. "Se trata de una obra de principiante, graciosa a veces, pero demasiado marcada por los giros y 'modos de hacer' de un 'vanguardismo' rebasado—aunque sus enfoques políticos, me jacto de ello, eran absolutamente correctos." *Recopilación*, p. 18.

14. The test is available in Frank Janney, *Alejo Carpentier and His Early Works* (London, 1981), pp. 125–32, and Benito Pelegrin, ed., *Alejo Carpentier et son oeuvre* (Paris, 1982), pp. 275-90, (hereafter Pelegrin, *Alejo Carpentier*). It has not been translated.

15. "El lenguaje deb[e] ajustarse en cada caso a la composición literia de la novela. Hay que llevar el lenguaje a sus extremas posibilidades de acuerdo con las exigencias del contenido." *Recopilación*, p. 45.

16. "Pensé, desde que empecé a tener una conciencia cabal de lo que quería hacer, que el escritor latinoamericano tenía el deber de "revelar" realidades inéditas. Y sobre todo salir del "nativismo", de "tipicismo", de la estampa pintoresca, para "desprovincializar" su literatura, elevándola a la categoría de valores universales." *Recopilación*, p. 19.

17. Janney, *Carpentier*, p. 125.

Chapter Two

1. "Sentí ardientemente el deseo de expresar el mundo americano. Aún no sabía cómo. Me alentaba lo difícil de la tarea por el desconocimiento de las esencias americanas. Me dediqué durante largos años a leer todo lo que podía sobre América, desde las Cartas de Cristóbal Colón, pasando por el Inca Garcilaso, hasta los autores del siglo dieciocho. Por espacio de casi ocho años creo que no hice otra cosa que leer textos americanos." *Recopilación*, p. 63.

2. Ibid.

3. First published in the Cuban magazine *Orígenes* 1, no. 4 (1944) and reproduced by Janney, *Carpentier*, pp. 120–24.

4. Klaus Müller-Bergh, " 'Oficio de tinieblas' un cuento escasamente conocido," in *Asedios a Carpentier*, ed. Klaus Müller-Bergh (Santiago de Chile, 1972), pp. 55–61, (hereafter *Asedios*).

5. Janney, *Carpentier*, p. 121.

6. Ibid., p. 105.

7. Lilia Pérez González, "El relato 'Los fugitivos' de Alejo Carpentier," *Papeles de San Armadans* 75 (1974):41–54.

8. Carlos Blanco Aguinaga, in *De mitologías y novelistas* (Madrid, 1975), pp. 120–21, writes persuasively on this point.

9. In *La novela latinoamericana en vísperas de un nuevo siglo y otros ensayos* (Mexico, 1981).

10. Irlmar Chiampi, *O realismo maravilhoso* (São Paulo: Editora Perspectiva, 1980), pp. 33–34.

11. " 'Viaje a la semilla' viene a ser una biografía tomada desde el momento de la muerte del personaje hasta el momento de su nacimiento. No es enteramente vano el juego si pensamos que una vida al reverso o al derecho tiene las mismas características al comienza como en su término . . . . Creo, en efecto, que mi relato titulado 'Viaje a la semilla,' es decir, el regreso a la madre, anuncia relatos futuros. Búsqueda de la madre o búsqueda del elemento primigenio en la matriz intelectual o telúrica." *Recopilación,* p. 26.

12. Manual Durán, "Viaje a la semilla," in *Asedios,* p. 74.

13. Jorge Luis Borges, *Otras inquisiciones,* in *Obras completas,* 2d ed. (Buenos Aires: Emecé, 1964), pp. 142–43.

14. Esther Mocega-González, *La narrativa de Alejo Carpentier* (New York, 1975), p. 50, fig. 2, and Pedro Ramírez Molas, *Tiempo y narración* (Madrid, 1978), p. 59.

15. "México, según una película europea," in *Crónicas* (Havana, 1976), 2:493.

16. *"El Cid Campeador* de Vincente Huidobro," in *Crónicas,* 1:189.

17. Roberto González Echevarría in Arrom, *Estudies,* p. 203.

18. "Manuel de Falla en París," in *Crónicas,* 1:180.

19. Carlos Rincón, "Textos desconocidos de Alejo Carpentier y Miguel Angel Asturias," *Actualidades* (Caracas) 2 (1977):97, 101.

20. *El reino de este mundo* (Santiago de Chile, 1969), p. 87. The subsequent quotation is from the same edition.

21. Ramírez Molas, *Tiempo,* p. 89.

22. *Recopilación,* p. 28.

23. Barreda Tomás, "Alejo Carpentier," p. 41, and Emir Rodríguez Monegal, "Lo real y lo maravilloso en *El reino de este mundo,"* in *Asedios,* p. 121.

Chapter Three

1. Emil Volek, "Dos cuentos de Carpentier: dos caras del mismo método artístico," *Nueva Narrativa Hispanoamericana* 1, no. 2 (1971):7.

2. *Orígenes* 9, no. 31 (1952).

3. See chapter 2, note 19 above.

4. "El hombre es a veces el mismo en diferentes edades y situarlo en su pasado puede ser tambien situarlo en su presente." *Recopilación,* p. 69.

5. "Je pense que l'homme a un comportement unique au milieu de circonstances changeantes. C'est ce que j'ai montré dans la nouvelle de *Guerra del tiempo* intitulée 'Semejante a la noche.' " Claude Fell, "Rencontre avec Alejo Carpentier," *Les Langues Modernes* 59, no. 3 (1965):106.

6. "Los hombre pueden flaquear, pero las ideas siguen su camino y encuentran al fin su aplicación." *Recopilación,* p. 69.

7. Roberto González Echevarría, *Relecturas* (Caracas, 1976), p. 64.

8. M. Roberto Assardo, " 'Semejante a la noche' o la contemporaneidad del hombre," in *Homenaje a Alejo Carpentier,* ed. Helmy F. Giacoman (New York, 1970), pp. 209–25, (hereafter Giacoman, *Homenaje*).

9. Graciela Maturo, "Religiosidad y liberación en *Ecue-Yamba-O* y *El reino de este mundo,*" in Zulma Palermo et al., *Historia y mito en la obra de Alejo Carpentier* (Buenos Aires, 1972), pp. 55–86.

10. González Echevarría, *Pilgrim at Home,* p. 106.

11. Hugo Rodríguez-Alcalá, "Sobre 'El camino de Santiago' de Alejo Carpentier," in Giacoman, *Homenaje,* pp. 243–59; Ariel Dorfman, *Imaginación y violencia en América* (Santiago de Chile, 1970), pp. 119–26.

12. Dorfman, *Imaginación,* p. 123.

13. David W. Foster, "The Everyman Theme in Alejo Carpentier's 'El camino de Santiago,' " *Symposium* 18 (1964):229–40. See also Ray Versasconi, "Juan y Sísifo en 'El camino de Santiago,' " in Zulma Palermo et al., *Historia y mito,* pp. 70–75, and Sharon Magnarelli, "El camino de Santiago," *Revista Iberoamericana* 40, no. 86 (1974):65–86.

14. "Debe advertirse, sin embargo, que a medida que transcurre el relato, Juan de Amberes se va transformando en un personaje que bien pudiera ser contemporáneo nuestro." Cited by González Echevarría, in Arrom, *Estudios* p. 209, and *Relecturas,* p. 83.

Chapter Four

1. "Y recuerdo que una tarde luminosa, extraordinaria, tuve algo así como una iluminación: la novela *Los pasos perdidos* nació en pocos segundos, completamente estructurada, hecha . . .," in *Alejo Carpentier, 75° aniversario,* unnumbered.

2. See, for example, among others, Luis Harss and Barbara Dohman, *Into the Mainstream* (New York, 1966), pp. 57–58, and Terry J. Peavler, "Alejo Carpentier and the Humanization of Latin-American Fiction," *Hispanófila* 74 (1982):68.

3. *Los pasos perdidos* (Barcelona, 1971), p. 111. Subsequent references are to this edition.

4. Ian R. Macdonald, "Magical Eclecticism: *Los pasos perdidos* and Jean Paul Sartre," in *Contemporary Latin American Fiction,* ed. Salvador Bacarisse (Edinburgh, 1980), p. 4.

5. Klaus Müller-Bergh, "Corrientes vanguardistas y surrealismo en las obras de Alejo Carpentier," in *Asedios,* p. 30.

6. "El final de mi novela, la moraleja, diríamos, afirma que el hombre para ser hombre y realizarse no puede escapar nunca a sus época,

aunque se le ofrezcan los medios para tal evasión." Cited by Emil Volek, "*Los pasos perdidos,*" *Universidad de la Habana* 189 (1968):25.

7. Roberto González Echevarría, "Ironía y estilo en *Los pasos perdidos,*" in *Relecturas,* pp. 37–51.

8. Volek, "Los pasos"; Eduardo González, *El tiempo del hombre* (Caracas, 1978); Susana Poujol, "Palabra y creación en *Los pasos perdidos,*" in Zulma Palermo et al., *Historia y mito en Alejo Carpentier; González Echevarría, Pilgrim at Home;* Zulma Palermo, "Aproximación a *Los pasos perdidos,*" in *Historia y mito;* and M. Ian Adams, *Three Authors of Alienation* (Austin, 1975).

9. Antonio Rodríguez Almodóvar, *La estructura de la novela burguesa* (Madrid, 1976), pp. 132–33.

10. King, *Carpentier,* pp. 15–19.

11. Müller-Bergh, *Carpentier,* p. 92.

12. González, *El tiempo,* p. 130.

Chapter Five

1. *El acoso,* in *Guerra del tiempo,* 1st ed. (Mexico City, 1958), p. 182. The following quotations are from the same edition.

2. Frances Weber, "Alejo Carpentier's War on Time," *Publications of the Modern Language Society of America* 78 (1963):444.

3. Ibid., p. 443.

4. Alberto J. Carlos, "El anti-héroe en *El acoso,*" in Giacoman, *Homenaje,* pp. 365–84, and Modesto Sánchez, "El fondo histórico de *El acoso,*" *Revista Iberoamericana* 41, nos. 92/3 (1975):397–438.

5. "Mi personaje central, huérfano de ideología, que actúa sin orientación precisa." "Carta," *Casa de las Américas* 125 (1981):71.

6. Emil Volek, "Análisis del sistema de estructuras musicales e interpretación de *El acoso* de Alejo Carpentier," in Giacoman, *Homenaje,* pp. 385–438; Edelweis Serra, "Estructura y estilo de *El acoso,*" in *Historia y mito en la obra de Alejo Carpentier* ed. Zulma Palermo, pp. 153–79; Esther Mocega-González, "La simbología religiosa en *El acoso* de Alejo Carpentier" in *Alejo Carpentier,* pp. 19–34.

7. *Afirmación literaria latinoamericana* (Caracas, 1978), pp. 22–23.

8. Graciela Maturo, "Religiosidad y liberación en *Ecue-Yamba-O* y *El reino de este mundo,*" in *Historia y mito,* pp. 85–86.

9. González Echevarría, *Pilgrim at Home,* p. 197, and Edelweis Serra, "Estructura," p. 160, respectively.

10. "Hoy ha sonado, para los cuentistas y novelistas de este continente, la hora difícil, gestatoria, decisiva, de empezar a encontrar, para sí mismos, expresiones nuevas, formas nuevas, nuevas soluciones a los problemas literarias. "La hora difícil," in *Letra y solfa,* comp. Alexis Márquez Rodríguez (Buenos Aires, 1976), p. 24.

11. González Echevarría, *Pilgrim at Home*, p. 218.
12. Angela B. Dellepiane, "Tres novelas de la dictadura," *Caravelle* 29 (1977):72.
13. Pamela E. Mason, "Indeterminism in Carpentier's *El derecho de asilo*," *Kentucky Romance Quarterly* 28 (1981):383–90; François Delprat, "La réflexion sur l'Histoire dans les nouvelles d'Alejo Carpentier," in Pelegrin, *Alejo Carpentier*, pp. 114–30.
14. Mason, "Indeterminism," p. 387.
15. Müller-Bergh, "Mito y realidad en 'Los advertidos,' " in Arrom, *Estudios*, p. 239.
16. "Los advertidos," in *Guerra del tiempo* (Barcelona, 1971), p. 138.
17. Antonio Fornet, "Sobre el tiempo y la historia en la obra de Alejo Carpentier," *Casa de las Américas* 129 (1981):68–73.

Chapter Six

1. "Los cánticos del progreso," in *Crónicas*, 2:510.
2. "En *El siglo de las luces* el personaje de Victor Hugues, positivo en un principio, se vuelve negativo al abrazar la causa del bonapartismo. Pero en el último capítulo quien triunfa es el pueblo de Madrid alzado contra Napoleón el día memorable fijado por Goya en su cuadro más famoso. Y, en fin de cuentas, fue de la Guadalupe gobernada por Victor Hugues de donde salió toda la propaganda que sirvió para encender la gran llamarada de las guerras de independencia de América." "Carta," *Casa de las Américas* 125 (1981):70–71.
3. *El siglo de las luces*, 1st ed. (Mexico, 1962), p. 222. Subsequent references are to this edition.
4. Jo Labanyi, "Nature and the Historical Process in Carpentier's *El siglo de las luces*," *Bulletin of Hispanic Studies* 57 (1980):55–66.
5. Claude Dumas, "*El siglo de las luces* de Alejo Carpentier, novela filosófica," in Giacoman, *Homenaje*, pp. 327–63.
6. Guillermo Morón, *Escritores latinoamericanos contemporáneos* (Caracas: Equinoccio, 1979), p. 74.
7. "Esteban tiene un terrible defecto y es que él es el utópico, el idealista que no tiene en realidad una conciencia política, ni un sentido. . . . [Es] . . . el intelectual que se hace una idea preconcebida de lo que debe ser una revolución, o la revolución, o su revolución, si es la de su país, y que apenas esa revolución se aparta de los esquemas preconcebidos por él, de acuerdo con una línea suya, inflexible, incapaz de seguir los meandros de los acontecimientos, empieza a perder pie, empieza a irritarse, empieza a no entender lo que ocurre y acaba en cierto modo renegando de lo que fue su ideal. Ese personaje lo hemos visto multiplicado por cien en todos los países del mundo, desde comienzos del siglo. Es

decir, el intelectual que se ajusta a una esquema." *Afirmación literaria,* p. 15 (my translation).

8. Labanyi, "Nature," p. 57.

9. "Sofía es todo lo contrario [de Esteban]. Sofía es la praxis. Sofía es la mujer que intuitivamente siente lo que hay que hacer y hacia dónde hay que ir. No le toca, desgraciadamente, vivir en un momento en que ella pueda dar su medida." *Afirmación literaria,* p. 15.

10. Mary A. Kilmer-Tchalekian, "Ambiguity in *El siglo de las luces*," *Latin American Literary Review* 4, no. 8 (1976):47–57, deals interestingly with the shifting narrative angle.

11. Mocega-González, *La narrativa de Alejo Carpentier,* p. 244. See in contrast Julio Ortega, "Sobre *El siglo de las luces,*" in *Asedios,* p. 202.

12. "En cuanto a Carlos, es sencillamente ese hombre dotado de un ideal. Hemos visto muchos de ellos—es el personaje menos interesante de la novela—, en que el ideal no le pasa de los 25 o 26 años, en que la necesidad de vivir, de ocuparse de su negocio, lo aburguesa. . . ." *Afirmación literaria,* p. 16.

13. Labanyi, "Nature," p. 56.

14. Ortega, "Sobre *El siglo,*" pp. 203–3

15. Dumas, *"El siglo,"* pp. 342–43.

Chapter Seven

1. "Oí las voces que habían vuelto a sonar, devolviéndome a mi adolescencia; escuché las voces nuevas que ahora sonaban, y creí que era mi deber poner mis energías, mis capacidades—si es que las tenía—al servicio del gran quehacer histórico latinoamericano que en mi país se estaba llevando adelante. . . . [E] n ese momento tuvimos todos la sensación de que podíamos ser útiles. Es lo que yo he llamado en in discurso, salir del período de la *soledad* para entrar en la etapa de la *solidaridad.*" *Razón de ser* (Caracas, 1976), pp. 23, 110.

2. "Siguiendo una larga tradición personal," ibid., p. 109.

3. José A. Portuondo, *La ciencia literaria* (Havana: Ministerio de Cultura, 1968), p. 31.

4. Judith Weiss, *Casa de las Américas* (Chapel Hill: University of North Carolina, 1968), p. 29.

5. "[E] 1 dictador latinoamericano es un producto tan característico del suelo americano que es necesario mostrar su realidad y tratar de desentrañar los enigmas de su reaparición periódica y casi continuada en el escenario latinoamericano. . . ." *Cuadernos para el Diálogo* (Madrid), 4 November 1976, p. 68.

6. *El recurso del método* (Havana, 1974), p. 98. Subsequent references are to this edition.

7. Maryse Vich-Campos, *"El recurso del método,"* in *"Caudillos", "Caciques" et dictateurs dans le roman hispano-americaine,* ed. Paul Verdevoye (Paris, 1978), p. 87. Cf. Christiane Baroche, "Alejo Carpentier et le temps suspendu," in Pelegrin, *Alejo Carpentier,* p. 38, who defines *El recurso del método* as "l'histoire d'un dictateur chassé par un dictateur en puissance" (the story of one dictator thrown out by a potential dictator).

8. Esther Mocega-González, "La evolución del personaje 'el estudiante' en tres relatos de Carpentier," in *Alejo Carpentier,* p. 109.

9. "El hombre que no acepta ese orden de cosas y avanza hacia el futuro," in *Recopilación,* p. 38.

10. "Si yo creyese que las abominables dictaduras que hoy padecen, en este siglo, muchos países de nuestro continente, constituyen [*sic*] un mal endémico, fatalmente latinoamericano, inseparable de nuestro destino continental, yo renegaría de mi condición de latinoamericano." *La novela latinoamericana en vísperas,* p. 19.

11. Ariel Dorfman, "Entre Proust y la momia americana: siete notas y un epílogo sobre *El recurso del método,"* *Revista Iberoamericana* 114, no. 5 (1981):95–128.

12. *Recopilación,* pp. 36–37.

13. Dorfman, "Entre Proust," 109–14.

Chapter Eight

1. "De una revelación privilegiada de la realidad, de una iluminación inhabitual o singularmente favorecedora de las inadvertidas riquezas de la realidad, de una ampliación de las escalas y categorías de la realidad, percibidas con particular intensidad en virtud de una exaltación del espíritu que lo conduce a un modo de 'estado límite.' " *Tientos y diferencias* (Mexico, 1964), p. 132.

2. "Lo hondo—lo realmente trascendental—de las cosas." Ibid., p. 11.

3. And in *La novela latinoamericana en vísperas de un nuevo siglo y otros ensayos.*

4. "Ejerciendo una suerte de chamanismo, es decir, de puesta en lenguaje audible de un mensaje que, en su origen, puede ser titubeante, informe, apenas enunciado y que llega al intérprete, al mediador, por bocanadas, por arranques, por aspiraciones. Jamás un término fue tan justo: recibir el mensaje de los movimientos humanos, comprobar su presencia, definir, describir, su actividad colectiva." *La novela latinoamericana en vísperas,* p. 47.

5. "Un especie de fiesta verbal," in *Afirmación literaria,* p. 28.

6. Renaud Richard, "Sur quelques aspects musicaux de la composition dans *Le siècle des lumières,"* in *Quinze études autour de El siglo de las luces de Alejo Carpentier,* ed. Daniel-Henri Pageaux (Paris, 1983), p. 60.

7. André Jansen, "Concierto barroco de Alejo Carpentier," *Cuadernos para investigación de la Literatura Hispánica* 2, no. 3 (1980):370–71.

8. *Concierto barroco* (Madrid, 1974), p. 81. The later reference is to this edition.

9. *Crisis* (Buenos Aires) 30 (1975):46.

10. *Triunfo* (Madrid) 779 (1977):19.

11. *La consagración de la primavera*, 4th ed. (Madrid, 1978), p. 230. Subsequent references are to this edition.

12. André Jansen, "¿Es *La consagración de la primavera* la obra maestra de Alejo Carpentier?", *Actas del 7° Congreso de la Asociación Internacional de Hispanistas*, ed. Giuseppe Bellini (Rome, 1982), pp. 591–601.

13. Angel Rama, "Los productivos años setenta de Alejo Carpentier," *Latin American Research Review* 16, no. 2 (1981):237.

14. See Donald L. Shaw, *Nueva narrativa hispanoamericana* (Madrid: Cátedra, 1981), p. 237.

15. *Triunfo* (Madrid) 981 (3 March 1980): 36.

16. André Saint Lu, "De quelques libertés du romancier avec l'histoire: à propos de *El arpa y la sombra* de Alejo Carpentier," *Les Langues Néo-Latines* 235 (1981):68–77, and "*La Harpe et l'Ombre:* Roman et histoire," in Pelegrin, *Alejo Carpentier,* pp. 90–102.

17. Jacques Leenhard, "Écrire l'histoire," ibid., pp. 77–89.

18. *El arpa y la sombra*, 2d ed. (Madrid, 1979), p. 187.

19. Jacqueline Tauzin, "*La Harpe et l'Ombre:* signification d'une structure," in Pelegrin, *Alejo Carpentier,* pp. 184–95.

Chapter Nine

1. Terry J. Peavler, "Alejo Carpentier and the Humanization of Latin American Fiction," *Hispanófila* 74 (1982):62.

2. Miguel Angel Asturias, *El Señor Presidente*, in *Obras completas* (Paris and Mexico: Klinksieck & Fondo de Cultura Económica, 1978) 3:159 (my translation).

3. "Personalmente, Vds lo saben, he tratado de especular a mi manera con el tiempo. Con el tiempo circular, regreso al punto de partida, es decir, un relato que se cierra sobre sí mismo, en *Los pasos perdidos,* y en *El Camino de Santiago.* El tiempo recurrente, o sea, el tiempo invertido, el tiempo en retroceso, en el *Viaje a la semilla.* El tiempo de ayer en hoy, es decir, un ayer significado presente en un hoy significante, en *El siglo de las luces,* en *El recurso del método,* en el *Concierto Barroco.* Un tiempo que gira en torno al hombre sin alterar su esencia en mi relato *Semejante a la noche. . . ."* *Razón de ser,* p. 94, and with slight alterations in *La novela latinoamericana en vísperas,* p. 156.

4. "Hay autonomía narrativa, sin interpretaciones, en autores como Julio Cortázar, Juan Rulfo, Carlos Fuentes, García Márquez, Roa Bastos

y yo. No podría decirse que hay entre nosotros, el peculiar 'aire de familia' que se observa entre los novelistas de la generación anterior." *La novela latinoamericana en vísperas,* p. 15.

5. Gerald Martin, "Vargas Llosa, nueva novela y realismo," *Norte* (Amsterdam) 12, nos. 5/6 (1971):112.

Selected Bibliography

PRIMARY SOURCES

1. Collections
Obras completas de Alejo Carpentier. Mexico: Siglo Veintiuno, 1983.
Cuentos completos. Barcelona: Bruguera, 1979.

2. Fiction
Ecue-Yamba-O. Madrid: Editorial España, 1933. Edition used: Barcelona: Bruguera, 1979.
Viaje a la semilla. Havana: Ucar García y Cía, 1944.
El reino de este mundo. Mexico: Edición y Distribución Iberoamericana de Publicaciones, 1949. Edition used: Santiago de Chile: Editorial Universitaria, 1969.
Los pasos perdidos. Mexico: Edición y Distribución Iberoamericana de Publicaciones, 1953. Edition used: Barcelona: Barral Editores, 1971.
El acoso. Buenos Aires: Editorial Losada, 1956. Edition used: *Guerra del tiempo.* Mexico: Compañía General de Ediciones, 1958.
Guerra del tiempo ("El Camino de Santiago," "Viaje a la semilla," "Semejante a la noche," and *El acoso*). Mexico: Compañía General de Ediciones, 1958. Some later editions omit *El acoso* and include "Los fugitivos" and "Los advertidos." Edition used: Barcelona: Barral Editores, 1971.
El siglo de las luces. Mexico: Compañía General de Ediciones, 1962.
El derecho de asilo. Barcelona: Editorial Lumen, 1972.
El recurso del método. Mexico: Siglo Veintiuno Editores, 1974. Edition used: Havana: Editorial de Arte y Literatura, 1974.
Concierto barroco. Mexico: Siglo Veintiuno Editores, 1974. Edition used: Madrid: Siglo Veintiuno Editores, 1981.
La consagración de la primavera. Mexico: Siglo Veintiuno Editores, 1978. Edition used: Madrid: Siglo Veintiuno Editores, 3d ed., 1978.
El arpa y la sombra. Mexico: Siglo Veintiuno Editores, 1979. Edition used: Madrid: Siglo Veintiuno Editores, 2d ed., 1979.

3. Nonfiction and essays
La música en Cuba. Mexico: Fondo de Cultura Económica, 1946.
Tientos y diferencias. Mexico: Universidad Nacional Autónoma, 1964. Amplified in later editions.

Razón de ser. Caracas: Universidad Central, 1976.
Afirmación literaria latinoamericana. Caracas: Universidad Central, 1978.
La novela latinoamericana en vísperas de un nuevo siglo y otros ensayos. Mexico:
    Siglo Veintiuno Editores, 1981.

4. Articles
Letra y solfa. Compiled by Alexis Márquez Rodríguez. Caracas: Síntesis
    Dos Mil, 1975.
Crónicas. 2 vols. Havana: Editorial Arte y Literatura, 1976.
Bajo el signo de La Cibeles. Compiled by Julio Rodríguez Puértolas. Madrid:
    Editorial Nuestra Cultura, 1979.
El adjetivo y sus arrugas. Buenos Aires: Editorial Galerna, 1980.
Ese músico que llevo dentro. 3 vols. Compiled by Zoila Gómez. Havana:
    Editorial Arte y Literatura, 1981.

5. Translations
The Lost Steps. Translated by Harriet de Onís. New York: Knopf, 1956.
The Kingdom of This World. Translated by Harriet de Onís. New York:
    Knopf, 1957.
Manhunt. Noonday 2 (1959): 109–80.
Explosion in a Cathedral. Translated by John Sturrock. Boston: Little,
    Brown, 1963.
War of Time. Translated by Frances Partridge. New York: Knopf, 1970.
Reasons of State. Translated by Frances Partridge. New York: Knopf, 1976.

SECONDARY SOURCES

1. Bibliography
González Echevarría, Roberto, and Müller-Bergh, Klaus. *Alejo Carpentier:
    Bibliographical Guide.* Westport, Conn.: Greenwood Press, 1983.

2. Books and parts of books
Adams, M. Ian. *Three Authors of Alienation: Bombal, Onetti, Carpentier.*
    Austin: University of Texas Press, 1975. Chapter 4 chiefly summa-
    rizes and comments on *Los pasos perdidos.*
Arias, Salvador (ed.). *Recopilación de textos sobre Alejo Carpentier.* Havana:
    Casa de las Américas, 1977. Contains important statements by Car-
    pentier and indispensible essays by major critics.
Barroso Octavo, Juan. *Realismo mágico y lo real maravilloso en El reino de este
    mundo y El siglo de las luces.* Miami: Universal, 1977. Useful for
    meanings attributed to Magical Realism and "lo real maravilloso";
    less good on the texts in question.

Blanco Aguinaga, Carlos. *De mitologías y novelistas.* Madrid: Turner Ediciones, 1975. Contains a discussion of Carpentier's positive view of myth (pp. 109–38).

Brushwood, John S. "El criollismo de esencias en *Don Goyo y Ecue-Yamba-O.*" In *Estudios de literatura hispanoamericana en honor a José J. Arrom,* edited by Andrew P. Debicki and Enrique Pupo-Walker, pp. 215–25. Chapel Hill: University of North Carolina Press, 1974. Argues that the two novels attribute positive value to belonging to a simple culture.

Diez Seijas, Pedro. "De la realidad al mito en *El siglo de las luces.*" In *La gran narrativa latinoamericana.* Caracas: Ediciones Nuevo Siglo, 1976. Contains a rather formalist essay with interesting comments on both meaning and structure (pp. 123–64).

Dorfman, Ariel. "El sentido de la historia en la obra de Alejo Carpentier." In *Imaginación y violencia en América.* Santiago de Chile: Editorial Universitaria, 1970. The author supports a noncircular view of Carpentier's outlook on history (pp. 93–137).

Durán Luzio, Juan. "El contexto histórico de *El recurso del método.*" In *Narradores latinoamericanos.* Edited by Oscar Sambrano Urdaneta. Caracas: Centro Rómulo Gallegos, 1980. Stresses the novel's relevance to all Latin America and proposes Tinoco of Costa Rica as a model for the central character (pp. 97–104).

Giacoman, Helmy F., ed. *Homenaje a Alejo Carpentier.* New York: Las Americas Publishing Co., 1970. Contains important statements by Carpentier and sixteen essays, many by leading critics.

González, Eduardo. *Alejo Carpentier: El tiempo del hombre.* Caracas: Monte Avila Editores, 1978. Includes versions of earlier published essays; very abstruse on the theme of time.

González Echevarría, Roberto. *Alejo Carpentier: The Pilgrim at Home.* Ithaca and London: Cornell University Press, 1977. The most stimulating and informative recent book.

———. "Alejo Carpentier." In *Narrativa y crítica de nuestra América,* edited by Joaquín Roy, pp. 127–60. Madrid: Editorial Castalia, 1978. A general survey of Carpentier's outlook and writings up to *Concierto barroco.*

———. "Notas para una cronología de la obra narrativa de Alejo Carpentier, 1944-1955." In *Estudios de literatura hispanoamericana en honor a José J. Arrom,* edited by Andrew P. Debicki and Enrique Pupo-Walker, pp. 201–14. Chapel Hill: University of North Carolina Press, 1974. Describes and attempts to date accurately works from "Oficio de tinieblas" to "El acoso."

———. *Relecturas.* Caracas: Monte Avila Editores, 1976. Contains: "Notas para una cronología de la obra narrativa de Alejo Carpentier" as in

Debicki and Pupo-Walker, *Estudios,* above (pp. 75–93); "Ironía y estilo en *Los pasos perdidos,*" on the function of irony as a distancing mechanism in the novel ((pp. 37–51); " 'Semejante a la noche' de Alejo Carpentier: historia/ficción," which carries the unconvincing suggestion that the real theme of the story is not time but its own narrative technique (pp. 53–73); and *"Concierto barroco* y las memorias del porvenir,*" which is based on the postulate that Carpentier's attitude to time changes in and after *El siglo de las luces* (pp. 153–59).

Harss, Luis, and Dohmann, Barbara. *Into the Mainstream.* New York: Harper & Row, 1966, 37–67. An interesting introduction to Carpentier's ideas and work up to *El siglo de las luces.*

Janney, Frank. *Alejo Carpentier and His Early Works.* London: Tamesis Books, Ltd., 1981. A helpful survey, especially of *Ecue-Yamba-O* and Carpentier's early style. The critical apparatus is occasionally inaccurate.

Kapschutschenko, Ludmila. *El laberinto en la narrativa hispanoamericana contemporánea.* London: Tamesis Books, Ltd., 1982. Chapter 3, "Alejo Carpentier: Búsqueda de lo perdido en el tiempo" (pp. 56–71), sees Time as a labyrinth in *Los pasos perdidos* and *Guerra del tiempo.*

King, Lloyd, *Alejo Carpentier, Caribbean Writer.* St. Augustine: University of the West Indies Press, 1977. The best short treatment in English. Full of new thought.

Macdonald, Ian. "Magical Eclecticism: *Los pasos perdidos* and Jean Paul Sartre." In *Contemporary Latin American Fiction.* Edited by Salvador Bacarisse. Edinburgh: Scottish Academic Press, 1980. Excellent on the narrator and on Sartrean elements in Carpentier's novel.

Marquez Rodríguez, Alexis. *La obra narrativa de Alejo Carpentier.* Caracas: Universidad Central, 1970. Very introductory, up to *El siglo de las luces.*

———. *El barroco y lo real maravilloso en la obra de Alejo Carpentier.* Mexico: Siglo Veintiuno Editores, 1982. The first book in Spanish to cover all Carpentier's work. Well documented on Carpentier but verbose and unscholarly.

Mecega-González, Esther. *La narrativa de Alejo Carpentier: el concepto del tiempo como tema fundamental.* New York: Eliseo Torres, 1975. Painstaking but largely content-descriptive. Covers only up to *El siglo de las luces.*

———. *Alejo Carpentier: estudios sobre su narrativa.* Madrid: Playor, 1980. Six essays especially useful on Carpentier's attitude to religion and to revolution.

Müller-Bergh, Klaus, ed. *Asedios a Carpentier.* Santiago de Chile: Editorial Universitaria, 1972. A fundamental collection of eleven essays by various critics.

―――. *Alejo Carpentier. Estudio Biográfico-crítico.* Long Island City, N.Y.: Las Americas Publishing Co., 1972. Chiefly useful for its detailed analysis of *Los pasos perdidos.*

―――. "Mito y realidad en 'Los advertidos.' " In *Estudios de literatura hispanoamericana en honor a José J. Arrom,* edited by Andrew P. Debicki and Enrique Pupo-Walker, pp. 239–56. Chapel Hill: University of North Carolina Press, 1974. Argues that the story reveals Carpentier's skeptical attitude toward historical progress.

Pageaux, Daniel-Henri, ed. *Quinze études autour de El siglo de las luces de Alejo Carpentier.* Paris: Éditions L'Harmattan, 1983. Some useful remarks on this novel but the standard of the essays is disappointing.

Palermo, Zulma, et al. *Historia y mito en la obra de Alejo Carpentier.* Buenos Aires: García Cambeiro, 1972. Has seven useful essays but some are flawed by eccentric interpretations of Carpentier's religious viewpoint.

Pelegrin, Benito, ed. *Alejo Carpentier et son oevre.* Paris: Sud, 1982. Eighteen essays chiefly interesting for those on *El arpa y la sombra.*

Ramirez Molas, Pedro. "El tiempo en el relato y el relato en el tiempo: Alejo Carpentier." In *Tiempo y narración.* Madrid: Gredos, 1978, 56–115. Deals with the treatment of time in "Viaje a la semilla," *Los pasos perdidos,* and *El siglo de las luces.*

Rodríguez Almodovar, Antonio. *La estructura de la novela burguesa.* Madrid: Taller de Ediciones, 1976. The *Segunda Parte* offers a rather hostile structuralist critique of Carpentier's general outlook and literary ideas and attempts to discuss his *retórica* (pp. 123–257).

Sanchez Boudy, José. *La temática novelística de Alejo Carpentier.* Miami: Universal, 1969. On Carpentier's ideas in his early work. Occasionally hostile. To be read with caution.

Smith, Verity. *Carpentier: Los pasos perdidos. A Critical Guide.* London: Grant & Cutler, 1983. A brief but incisive introduction to the problems of this text.

Sommers, Joseph. "*Ecue-Yamba-O:* Semillas del arte narrativo de Alejo Carpentier." In *Estudios de literatura hispanoamericana en honor a José J. Arrom,* edited by Andrew P. Debicki and Enrique Pupo-Walker, pp. 227–38. A general discussion of the novel emphasizing Carpentier's irony and detached skepticism.

Souza, Raymond D. *Major Cuban Novelists: Innovation and Tradition.* Colombia and London: Missouri University Press, 1976. Chapter 2, "Alejo Carpentier's Timeless History" (pp. 30–52), contains a descriptive survey of Carpentier's fiction up to *El siglo de las luces.*

Speratti-Piñero, Emma S. *Pasos hallados en El reino de este mundo.* Mexico: El Colegio de Mexico, 1981. Very informative on the historical background and sources of the novel.

Vich-Campos, Maryse. "El recurso del método." In *"Caudillos," "Caciques" et dictateurs dans le roman hispano-américaine.* Edited by Paul Verdevoye. Paris: Éditions Hispaniques, 1978. Attmpts, inter alia, to relate its treatment of Time to the prevailing view of Carpentier's outlook.

Vila Selma, José. *El "último" Carpentier.* Las Palmas: Mancomunidad de Cabildos, 1978. Polemical and highly personal. Chiefly on *El recurso del método* and *Concierto barroco.*

Young, Richard A. *Carpentier: El reino de este mundo. A Critical Guide.* London: Grant & Cutler, 1983. A short but pithy review of the main features of the text.

3. Articles

Acosta, Leonardo. "El Almirante segun don Alejo." *Casa de las Américas* 121 (1980):26–40. On Carpentier's use of sources and his interpretation.

Alonso, Carlos J. "Viaje a la semilla." *Modern Language Notes* 94 (1979):386–93. Sees it polemically as destroying the literary postulates implicit in *El reino de este mundo.*

Armas, Frederick A. "Metamorphosis as Revolt: Cervantes' *Persiles y Segismunda* and Carpentier's *El reino de este mundo.*" *Hispanic Review* 49 (1981):297–316. Suggests the *Persiles* as a source; interesting on the ambiguity of the "marvelous."

Ayora, Jorge. "La alienación marxista en *Los pasos perdidos.*" *Hispania* 57 (1974):886–92. Opens an interesting perspective on the narrator's outlook.

Barreda-Tomás, Pedro M. "Alejo Carpentier: dos visiones del negro, dos conceptos de la novela." *Hispania* 55 (1972):34–44. Explores the contrasts he sees in Carpentier's first two novels.

Bell, Steven M. "Carpentier's *El reino de este mundo* in a New Light: Towards a Theory of the Fantastic." *Journal of Spanish Studies: Twentieth Century* 8 (1980):29–43. A handy contribution to the debate around the idea of "lo real maravilloso."

Bockus Aponte, Barbara. "La creación del espacio literario en *El recurso del método.*" *Revista Iberoamericana* 96, no. 7 (1976):567–72. Studies the alternation between Paris and Latin America in the novel.

Castellanos, J., and Martínez, M.A. "El dictador latinoamericano como personaje literario." *Latin American Research Review* 16, no. 2 (1981):79–105. More general than Dellepiane's article below, but useful for context.

Dellepiane, Angela B. "Tres novelas de la dictadura: *El recurso del método, El otoño del patriarca, Yo, el Supremo.*" *Caravelle* 29 (1977):65–87. Chiefly on the ambivalence of Carpentier's dictator, in the relevant section.

Donohue, Francis. "Alejo Carpentier: la preocupación del tiempo." *Cuadernos Hispanoamericanos* 202 (1966):141–51. Postulates four different approaches to Time in *Guerra del tiempo.*

Dorfman, Ariel. "Entre Proust y la momia americana: siete notas y un epilogo sobre *El recurso del método.*" *Revista Iberoamericana* 114, no. 5 (1981):95–128. A penetrating analysis of important feature of the text.

Durán Luzio, Juan. "Un nuevo epílogo a la historia: *El arpa y la sombra* de Alejo Carpentier." *Casa de las Américas* 125 (1981):100–110. Interesting comments on Carpentier's uses of irony and his point of view.

Fell, Claude. "Rencontre avec Alejo Carpentier." *Les Langues Modernes* 59, no. 3 (1965):101–8. An important early interview. For others see Janney, cited above, p. 135, and chapter 8 of the present work, notes 9 and 10.

Fornet, Ambrosio. "Sobre el tiempo y la historia en la obra de Alejo Carpentier." *Casa de las Américas* 129 (1981):68–73. Criticises what he sees as misunderstandings by other critics and presents a dualistic view.

Foster, David William. "The Everyman Theme in Alejo Carpentier's 'El Camino de Santiago.' " *Symposium* 18 (1964):229–40. Highly perceptive in terms of the tale's universal meaning.

García Castro, Ramón. "La pintura en *Los convidados de piedra, Concierto Barroco* y *El recurso del método.*" *Revista Iberoamericana* 110/111 (1980):67–84. Reviews the various references in detail.

Giordano, Jaime. "Unidad estructural en Alejo Carpentier." *Revista Iberoamericana* 75 (1971):391–401. Works outward from subchapter 34 of *El siglo de las luces.*

Gullón, Germán. "El narrador y la narración en *Los pasos perdidos.*" *Cuadernos Hispanoamericanos* 263, no. 64 (1972):501–9. Extremely useful on the duality of the narrator and on the perspectivism in the narrative of this work.

Jansen, André. "Concierto barroco de Alejo Carpentier." *Cuadernos para Investigación de la Literatura Hispánica* 2, no. 3 (1980): 369–73. Analyzes the author's aims in the book.

———. "¿Es *La consagración de la primavera* (1978) la obra maestra de Alejo Carpentier?" *Actas del 7° Congreso de la Asociación Internacional de Hispanistas.* Edited by Giuseppe Bellini, Rome: Bulzoni, 1982, pp. 591–601. Sees the novel as a compendium of Carpentier's ideas and ideals.

Kilmer-Tchalekian, Mary. "Ambiguity in *El siglo de las luces.*" *Latin American Literary Review* 4, no. 8 (1976):47–57. Very perceptive on the shifting narrative point of view.

Labanyi, Jo. "Nature and the Historical Process in Carpentier's *El siglo de las luces.*" *Bulletin of Hispanic Studies* 57 (1980):55–66. Perhaps the best single essay on a central theme of the text.

Magnarelli, Sharon. " 'El Camino de Santiago' de Alejo Carpentier y la picaresca." *Revista Iberoamericana* 86 (1974):65–86. Advocates a purely literary reading.

Mason, Patricia E. "Indetermination in Alejo Carpentier's 'El derecho de asilo.' " *Kentucky Romance Quarterly* 28 (1981):383–90. Interprets cogently Carpentier's use of tenses.

Mujica, Hector. "Alejo Carpentier y la responsibilidad del escritor." *Casa de las Américas* 129 (1981):57–73. A "committed" defense of Carpentier as a "committed" writer.

Osopat, Lev. "El hombre y la historia en la obra de Alejo Carpentier." *Casa de las Américas* 87 (1974):9–20, and 125 (1981):72–82. The first article discusses the treatment of history in *El reino de este mundo* and *El siglo de las luces,* the second is rather more on the role of the narrator in *Los pasos perdidos.*

Peavler, Terry J. "The source for the Archetype in *Los pasos perdidos.*" *Romance Notes* 15 (1974):58–87. Suggests Poe's Arthur Gordon Pym.

———. "A New Novel by Alejo Carpentier." *Latin American Literary Review* 3, no. 6 (1975):31–36. Makes useful points about *El recurso del método.*

———. "*Alejo Carpentier and the Humanization of Latin-American Fiction.*" *Hispanófila* 74 (1982):61–78. Discusses the evolution of Carpentier's characterization.

Pérez-González, Lilia. "El relato 'Los fugitivos' de Alejo Carpentier." *Papeles de San Armadans* 75 (1974):41–54. Stresses the theme of return to the source.

Piedra, José. "A Return to Africa with a Carpentier Tale." *Modern Language Notes* 97 (1982):401–10. Discusses the "African substratum" in "Histoire de Lunes." The interpretation that follows is perhaps questionable.

Pontiero, Giovanni. "The Human Comedy in El reino de este mundo." *Journal of Inter-American Studies* 12 (1970):527–38. On Carpentier's "theatrical" narrative manner.

Rama, Ángel. "Los productivos años setenta de Alejo Carpentier." *Latin American Research Review* 16 (1981):224–45. Outspoken on earlier criticism and on *La Consagración de la Primavera* and *El arpa y la sombra.*

Rincón, Carlos. "Textos desconocidos de Alejo Carpentier y Miguel Angel Asturias." *Actualidades* (Caracas) 2 (1977):95–105. Reproduces the 1944 "Capítulo de la novela," which was to develop into part of *El reino de este mundo.*

Sánchez, Modesto. "El fondo histórico de *El acoso.*" *Revista Iberoamericana* 92, no. 3 (1975):397–442. Enlightening on the politico-historical background.

Saint-Lu, André. "De quelques libertés du romancier avec l'histoire: à propos de *El arpa y la sombra.*" *Les Langues Neo-Latines* 235 (1980):68– 77. Elucidates a number of important instances.

Speratti-Piñero, Emma S. "Noviciado y apoteosis de Ti Noel en *El reino de este mundo* de Alejo Carpentier." *Bulletin Hispanique* 80, nos. 3/4 (1978):201–28. A preview of her book, but more specifically on Ti Noel and Haitian Negro beliefs.

Townsend, Lindsay, "The Image of Art in *Los pasos perdidos* and *El acoso.*" *Romance Notes* 20 (1980):304–9. Discusses the significance of the Eroica symphony.

Volek, Emil. "Los pasos perdidos." *Universidad de La Habana* 189 (1968):25– 37. Makes interesting remarks on structure.

Weber, Frances Wyers. *"El acoso:* Alejo Carpentier's War on Time." *Publications of the Modern Languages Association of America* 78 (1963):440– 48. The best article on this text. Practically all subsequent criticism on it simply develops Weber's ideas.

Index

Abela, Eduardo, 17
Adams, M. Ian, 53
Aeschylus, 57
Afro-Cubanism, 4, 5, 8, 9, 10, 42, 106
Apollinaire, Guillaume, 16
Arguedas, José María, 4, 124
Arlt, Roberto, 3
Armstrong, Louis, 106, 108
Asturias, Miguel Ángel, 4, 124
Azuela, Mariano, 2, 16

Balzac, Honoré de, 1
Barreda Tomás, Pedro, 34
Barrios, Eduardo, 2
Batista, Fulgencio, 93, 111, 112
Beethoven, Ludwig von, 47, 57, 58, 60
Bloy, Léon, 120, 122
Boeklin, Arnaldo, 16
Bontempelli, Massimo, 16
Borges, Jorge Luis, 3, 25
Breton, André, 17, 110

Carlos, A. J., 60
Carpentier, Alejo: American roots, 15; appraisal, 124–27; attitude toward reality, 62, 82, 87, 125–26; attitude toward time and history, 40, 61, 69, 72–73, 74, 87, 92, 107, 117, 123; contacts with surrealism, 12, 17; early life, 1–2; fictional theory, 100–104; journalism, 1–2, 15–17; marriage, 43; musical interests, 15, 18; Parisian period, 11, 15, 43; pessimism about Europe, 43, 47; political attitudes, 2, 11, 58, 64, 72, 78, 79, 80, 88, 92, 93, 97, 107, 109, 111–12, 116–18, 122; religious themes, 37, 70, 78–81, 85–86, 113; return to Cuba (1939) 43, (1959) 88; theory of the Marvelous Real, 21–23, 51; trip to Haiti, 27, 44; trips to interior of Venezuela, 44, 45; trip to Mexico, 35

WORKS—BALLET SCENARIOS:
"Milagro de Anaquillé, El," 5, 6
"Rebambaramba, La," 5

WORKS—PROSE:
Acoso, El, 19, 38, 40, 57–65, 69, 75, 76, 78, 81, 82, 88, 90, 109, 127
"Advertidos, Los," 40, 70, 71–73
Arpa y la sombra, El, 44, 119–23
"Camino de Santiago, El," 38–42, 70, 125
Clan disperso, El, 15, 35, 44, 45, 109
Concierto barroco, 22, 65, 104–108, 125
Consagración de la primavera, La, 65, 69, 75, 86, 88, 89, 93, 98, 99, 102, 104, 107, 108–19, 124, 125
Derecho de asilo, El, 65–71, 94
Ecue-Yamba-O, 2–6, 6–11, 12, 13, 14, 15, 16, 20, 22, 26, 28, 30, 33, 34, 37, 89, 90, 110, 119
"Fugitivos, Los," 17, 19–21, 23
Guerra del tiempo, 19, 35, 36, 65, 71
"Histoire de lunes," 11–14, 15, 20, 22
Música en Cuba, La, 16, 18, 35, 39, 40, 44
"Oficio de tinieblas," 17, 18–19, 20, 22, 25, 35
Pasos perdidos, Los, 3, 20, 23, 24, 26, 31, 38, 43–45, 45–56, 57, 61, 71, 75, 86, 88, 90, 93, 96, 98, 123, 125
Razón de ser, 102
Recurso del método, El, 15, 31, 65, 66, 67, 69, 71, 75, 78, 89–99, 105, 108, 109, 110, 111, 119, 121, 123, 125
Reino de este mundo, El, 13, 15, 17, 18, 19, 22, 23, 26–34, 35, 37, 39, 42, 44, 53, 75, 88, 90, 100, 101, 104, 108, 118
"Semejante a la noche," 35–38, 39, 125
Siglo de las luces, El, 15, 20, 32, 33, 36, 39, 53, 61, 65, 69, 72, 74–87, 88, 89, 90, 91, 94, 97, 108, 109, 110, 111, 114, 118, 125
Tientos y diferencias, 26, 102, 103
"Viaje a la semilla," 22, 23–26, 104, 125
"Visión de América," 44

Carrión, Miguel de, 4
Carteles, 1, 43, 71, 74, 127

148